Cyber Careers

Cyber Careers

The Basics of Information Technology and Deciding on a Career Path

Pee Vululleh, PhD

CRC Press is an imprint of the
Taylor & Francis Group, an **informa** business

First Edition published 2022
by CRC Press
6000 Broken Sound Parkway NW, Suite 300, Boca Raton, FL 33487-2742

and by CRC Press
4 Park Square, Milton Park, Abingdon, Oxon, OX14 4RN

CRC Press is an imprint of Taylor & Francis Group, LLC

Library of Congress Cataloging-in-Publication Data
A catalog record has been requested for this book

ISBN: 978-1-032-06843-5 (hbk)
ISBN: 978-1-032-06844-2 (pbk)
ISBN: 978-1-003-20411-4 (ebk)

DOI: 10.1201/9781003204114

Typeset in Caslon
by SPi Technologies India Pvt Ltd (Straive)

Contents

1

Introduction to Information Technology

1.1 Introduction

Information technology is not a new thing; it has been around for a long time. Humans have always found ways to communicate better and faster, adapting technology to suit the communication styles of their specific age and generation. During the pre-mechanical period, for instance, people used simple pictures to map territories, tell stories, and so on. The Information Age (or Digital Age) introduced computer technology to disseminate information easily, quickly, and widely. This chapter introduces students to the basic definition of information technology.

1.2 What is Information Technology?

So what is information technology?

For many people, the phrase *information technology* or *IT* involves the person you call when your computer has a problem. While that view of IT is not entirely wrong, it understates the scope of this critical career field. If you are not in the field of IT yourself, you might not know and understand just how IT affects your life. To better grasp information technology, you must first define each term (*information* and *technology*) separately. Knowing the meaning of each will then give you a better understanding of their combined meaning. Let us begin with the term *information.*

1.2.1 What is Information?

Information is processed data on which our decisions and actions are based. Data are the raw material like numbers or words (see Figure 1.1). Whereas data are the collection of facts, information is how you

DOI: 10.1201/9781003204114-1

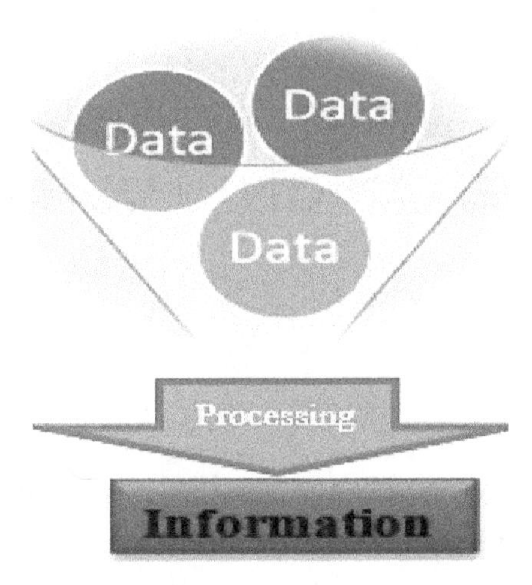

Figure 1.1 Transforming data into information.

understand those facts in context. Data are unorganized, while information is organized. In the context of computers, data are the input (i.e., what you tell the computer to do). Information is the output (i.e., the computer interpretations of the inputted data and its outcome).

For a decision to be meaningful, the processed data must meet three criteria: accuracy, completeness, and timeliness (ACT).

Accuracy. Information should be based on correct, complete data and be free from bias. Accuracy is essential as decision-makers must be able to rely on the information to make the right decision. For example, suppose government statistics based on the last census wrongly show an increase in births within an area. In that case, plans may be made by businesses to invest more in the area. Such actions may yield no fruit for the involved companies in part due to the inaccurate information.

Completeness. Information should contain all the required details; otherwise, it may not be useful as the basis for decision-making. Information should be complete, meaning that facts and figures should not be missing or concealed. For example, suppose a company is provided with information regarding the costs of supplying a fleet of cars for sales, but servicing and maintenance costs are omitted. Cost calculation based on this information will be underestimated. Telling the truth but not wholly is of no use.

Timeliness. Information should be available when required. Information received too late will be irrelevant. Suppose you receive a brochure and notice that your favorite basketball team played yesterday; by then the information is too late to be of use. Going to watch your favorite team for that game will not be an option because the game day and time have passed. Information should be given or received on time. A report to your managers that is three weeks late is most likely useless. To be useful, the information should have been received at or before the deadline to be included in the managers' decision-making process.

1.2.2 The Need for Information

Information is a requirement for carrying out an organization's decision-making activities. The successful flow of activities in a business depends on the quality of the information. Information provides context for data. It improves our knowledge, thereby enabling us to make decisions and initiate actions.

Dates provide a simple example insofar as they are meaningless without the information that makes those dates relevant. Examples of information would include that January 1 is New Year's Day, or that December 25 is Christmas day. Figure 1.1 presents the raw data/facts which go through processing. The processing includes guidelines and procedures used to select, organize, and manipulate data to suit a specific task. Finally, it produces information, a collection of facts organized to have additional value beyond the value of the constituent facts.

1.2.3 What is Technology?

The role played by technology and its impact on both our personal and working lives are ever-growing. *Technology* is one of our world's keywords, yet it is also one of the most confused. It is defined as the set of skills, knowledge, experience, and techniques through which we change, transform, and use our environment to invent useful tools that meet our needs and desires. Technology involves a specific physical form of information and knowledge such as drawings, blueprints, models, diagrams, and sketches or non-physical form such as technical services. Technology comprises mechanisms for disseminating messages that, in turn, help us save time and energy by providing convenience at work—for example, radio and television broadcasting, telephony, computer networks, and satellites. Technology is used to produce goods and services that are considered useful in computers, machines, and medicines.

Examples of technology include the Internet, which allows people to improve the quality of their lives. Ultrasound imaging devices, as used in healthcare, enable doctors to see inside the human body. Electronic learning (e-learning) used in education allows students to learn anytime and without being restricted to a particular location. To participate in an online course, you must use technology. Online courses involve posting in discussion forums, submitting assignments, or taking tests. All these are done online using technology such as a computer, the Internet, and so on. Video, cell phones, and equipment used to create, document, and analyze information are also considered technology.

The word *technology* suggests that it is a means to an end. For example, a car is a means of transportation. The goal of car driving is to reach a destination. Using matches is a means of creating a fire. The end is the fire itself. When we talk about technology, we must always remember that it is a means, not an end. In the broadest sense, technology is about taking action to meet human needs. For example, the invention of the microscope was driven by a need to explore tiny things. This technological solution has allowed us to understand other things in the world that, in turn, have made our lives easier and led to the development of other advanced technologies.

1.2.4 Information Technology Defined

So, now, what is information technology?

Information technology is a combination of information and technology. IT is a subset of information systems (IS). IT is the technology aspect of systems themselves. Whereas IS incorporates the technology, people, and processes involved with technology, IT is the design and implementation of information within IS. In other words, IT can be defined as the study and use of systems (telecommunications and computers) for storing, retrieving, and sending information

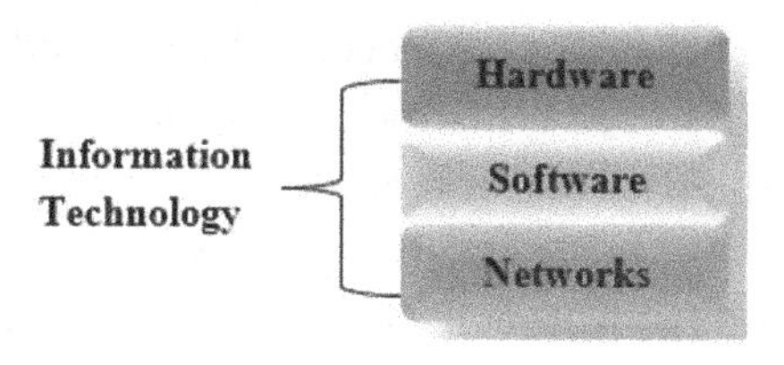

Figure 1.2 Information technology components.

in various forms to different persons and places. Typically, IT includes hardware, software, and networks (see Figure 1.2), which are further discussed in Chapters 2, 3, and 4. IT is responsible for protecting an organization's information, processing the information, transmitting the information, and retrieving it.

To protect an organization's valuable data, IT helps store the organization's important data and protects them from unauthorized disclosure. For example, a storage system, such as vaults, can help keep information safe by only allowing certain users within a company to access, make changes, or withdraw documents. IT focuses on managing technology and improving its use to advance the overall business goals.

Information technology, therefore, is not limited to the following:

- Managing a network of computers
- Providing technical support
- Coding and decoding software

Examples of information technology are:

- Network communications equipment such as bridges, routers, and hubs
- Computers used by teachers and students for educational purposes
- The Internet used to browse for information

1.3 Origins of Information Technology

Humans have been using and advancing technology to meet their needs for a long time. In 1945, the development of a stored program concept allowed programs to be read into a computer. The significance of this achievement may not have been fully realized at the time, but the potential for IT increased tremendously because of it. This development has laid the basis for unprecedented achievements ever since. The term *information technology* did not appear until the mid-20th century, which saw the influx of early office technology. *The Harvard Business Review* first published the term *IT* in 1958.

The driving force behind continual advancement in information technology is the human desire to store, recover, and share as much information as possible both quickly and easily. The bottom line is that IT will be around for a long time—as long as humans exist. Ignoring IT opportunities or failing to address the problems threatening its advancement will do us no good. That is why understanding IT and its many facets is necessary for anyone interested in moving forward in today's fast-paced society.

1.4 The Internet

Remember that technology is the end product to which users have access, such as WhatsApp, software applications, and so on. Information technology is about more than just the computer itself. It as well involves storing, retrieving, or manipulating data. A notable achievement that led to modern IT was the development of the World Wide Web, a collection of web pages found on the Internet (a computer network).

The Internet is like the roads that connect cities and towns. The World Wide Web, on the other hand, is like the shops, gas stations, and houses you would see on those roads. Cars on the road can be likened to the data—going between websites or transferring files across the Internet separately from the Web. The Internet is what people use to share information and communicate from anywhere with an internet connection. It is a vast network of interconnected computers. The Internet facilitates communication from one website to another website. IT is the study of using technology as a means of sending, receiving, and displaying information in more simple terms. Basically, the Internet is a giant server where information is stored for retrieval using various programming languages, databases, and hyperlinks. The Internet is not owned by anyone, although various organizations collaborate in its development and functioning. However, various telephone companies own high-speed cables through which internet data pass.

1.5 The Purpose of Information Technology

IT has many purposes. IT is used to improve any individual or business organization's operations by enhancing information processing and dissemination. IT is used to help organizations achieve profitable results and keep competitive forces in check. IT is also used to optimize the effectiveness and efficiency of processes within business organizations. In both educational and business contexts, IT is used to solve problems (which is further discussed in Chapter 8).

Furthermore, IT provides supporting information to assist managers in decision-making. IT offers effective communication and allows the effective management of information. In traditional marketing, for instance, managers are required to physically find an audience, discover their needs, and build a marketing campaign to suit them. However, the use of technology (mainly internet marketing) enables managers to use online advertising methods such as Facebook ads and search engine optimization (SEO) to achieve the same goal in the fastest possible time. Knowing the exact number of people who may have seen an ad in a newspaper is difficult, but it is easy to determine out how many people clicked on an online banner. SEO improves an organization's website by increasing its visibility for closely connected searches. The better the visibility the pages have in search results, the better they are to garner attention and attract prospective and existing customers.

1.6 Chapter Summary

Information technology is the study and use of systems (telecommunications and computers) for storing, retrieving, and sending information in various forms to different persons and places. IT includes hardware, software, and networks. IT is responsible for protecting an organization's information as well as processing, transmitting, and retrieving the information. IT helps store an organization's important data and protects them from unauthorized disclosure. The bottom line is that IT will be around for a long time—as long as humans exist.

Chapter Review Questions

1. What is information? What are its prerequisites?
2. Explain the need of information in our lives.
3. What is technology? Give some examples of areas where technology is being used.
4. How can data become information?
5. Explain in your own words the advantages and impact of IT in our lives.
6. Give one reason behind the continual advancement in IT.
7. Suppose a friend asks you to explain the concept of information technology. How would you define it? Write a one-paragraph description in your own words that you feel would best describe your friends' information technology.

Multiple Choice Questions

8. Which of the following is not a technology?
   A. Internet
   B. Blue-ray players
   C. Flag
   D. Laptop
9. Which of the following is not a technology?
   A. Interactive Whiteboards
   B. Tree
   C. Video Camera
   D. Robotics
10. "Number" is an example of
    A. Information
    B. Data
    C. Technology
    D. Both A & C
11. Processed data are an example of
    A. Data
    B. Information
    C. Process
    D. All the Above

12. Which of the following is an attribute of information?
    A. Timeliness
    B. Accuracy
    C. Relevancy
    D. All of these
13. What are the three components that make up IT?
    A. Hardware, Software, Polices
    B. Hardware, Software, People
    C. Hardware, Software, Networks
    D. Hardware, Software, Process
14. Age is an example of
    A. Information
    B. IT
    C. Processes
    D. Data

True or False

15. Information refers to the raw data.
    True
    False
16. The processed data are called data.
    True
    False
17. The processed data are called Information Technology.
    True
    False
18. The processed data are called information.
    True
    False
19. Data are organized facts.
    True
    False
20. Data are considered to be the output, while information is the input.
    True
    False

21. Information & Data come with different meanings.
    True
    False
22. The abbreviation WWW stands for Word Wide Web.
    True
    False

Fill in the Blanks

23. ________is data that has been transformed into an output that is valuable to users.
24. ________consists of unstructured facts.
25. ________is the combination of hardware and software that people use to communicate or share information.
26. ________is accessing learning electronically.
27. Your web browser uses the ________ to access the web.
28. ________ is a vast network of computers all connected.
29. ________ is a wide network that allows computer networks around the world to talk to one another.
30. The components of IT include ________, software, and ________.

2
Hardware

2.1 Introduction

Technology is increasingly becoming a necessity rather than a mere utility. Technology helps families communicate in different countries, allows businesses to conduct worldwide transactions, and is the future of entertainment. This level of connectedness is achieved due to the highly symbiotic nature of hardware for creating functional user experiences. While several other things are necessary and integral, this chapter will focus on the hardware that powers these great devices.

2.2 Hardware

Hardware encompasses the physical (visible) technology that works with information. In other words, hardware is any part, component, or device related to technology and its networks that you can physically touch. We can use the simple analogy of riding a bike (Figure 2.1). The bike and your body are the hardware. The chain and the pedals move the wheels, the handlebars steer, and the body provides the motive force and fine-tuning for navigation. Hardware can be as

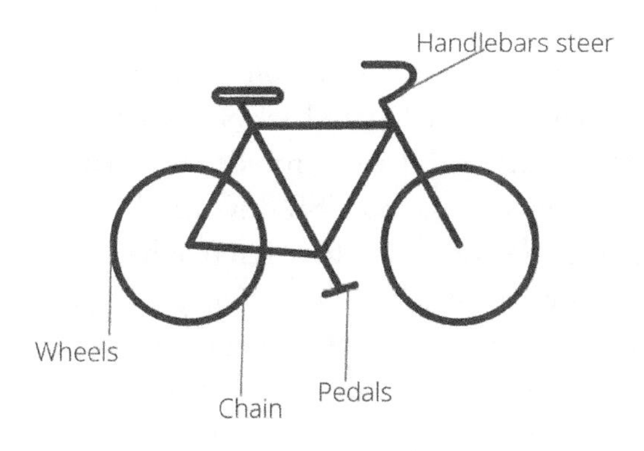

Figure 2.1 Bike analogy.

DOI: 10.1201/9781003204114-2

Figure 2.2 Computer hardware.

small as a cell phone in your pocket or as large as a supercomputer that fills an entire room.

In a computing context, hardware is the collection of physical elements that comprise a computer system, such as computer monitors, keyboards, mouse, and so on (Figure 2.2). Hardware can be distinguished from software. Anything physical related to the computer is considered hardware, while anything nonphysical that makes the computer function—such as the operating system and applications—are considered software. Computer hardware receives directions from the software before executing any instructions or commands. (Software is further explained in Chapter 3.)

It is important to note that different hardware types serve different purposes, but external hardware devices and internal hardware devices are the two most common types. The external hardware devices are referred to as *peripheral*, while the internal hardware parts are referred to as *components.*

External hardware devices are those that are installed outside of the computer. For example, a printer is considered an external hardware device because it is connected to the back of the computer and is outside of the case. Other external devices include monitors, keyboards, CD/DVD drives, floppy drives, and USB drives and scanners. Almost all forms of external hardware parts have internal hardware components.

Internal hardware parts are those that go inside the computer. Without these crucial components, computers would not be able to function. Almost all electronic devices include a power supply, motherboard, central processing unit (CPU), random-access memory (RAM), storage, graphics card, sound card, network card, and cooling unit. Each of these components has vital functions.

2.2.1 Random-Access Memory

Random-Access Memory (RAM) is a form of internal hardware that is used to store and process information. This device stores and retrieves the computer's most critical information. RAM is responsible for loading things such as the operating system during the computer's booting process. RAM is volatile, meaning that it requires power to function. Compared to other storage whereby data are stored and accessed sequentially, RAM is accessed randomly and without any sequence—as the name implies. The speed that a RAM uses in processing data is faster than that of a hard disk. However, it is known to be an explosive device if the computer system gets shut down, meaning that all information stored gets wiped out of the RAM. A hard disk, on the other hand, keeps data permanently as it is non-volatile. RAM is mainly available in two different types: Dynamic random-access memory (DRAM) and static random-access memory (SRAM). SRAM is used within a CPU's cache memory, while DRAM is utilized in modern computers.

2.2.2 Hard Disk

The hard disk is another component of computer hardware that stores data. It can be preinstalled within the computer processing unit or might be used as an external device.

The hard disk is considered a non-volatile component, meaning that data are permanently stored within it and is not wiped out if there is a system shut down. The hard disk comprises a surface that electromagnetically stores data in high chunks and can be easily accessed. It has the capability of storing trillions of data bytes. The hard disk's internal component contains a stacked disk collection with electromagnetic surfaces within which data are stored.

2.2.3 Graphics Card

The graphics or video card is primarily tasked with processing images and video. While some CPUs have an integrated graphics part, many desktop PCs and all gaming pcs include an external graphics card, as video rendering is a very intensive process. It is common now that external graphics cards have their only video RAM explicitly used to load these power-hungry videos and graphics.

2.2.4 Monitor

The monitor is a computer hardware component used to display the videos, output, and additional graphics since it is connected directly to the CPU. Any video that is to be displayed via the monitor makes use of a video card. The monitor is like a television set. However, the difference is in the graphics. The resolutions that a monitor displays tend to be of a much higher quality than that of television.

A desktop computer is usually linked to the monitor through a cable and is fitted with a video card within the computer system motherboard. In the case of tablets and laptops, the monitor tends to be pre-built within the system, and no separate hardware is installed within these gadgets.

2.2.5 Central Processing Unit

A central processing unit (CPU), also referred to as a processor or the computer's brain, is the bridge between the hardware and software. The CPU's primary function is to take input from a peripheral (keyboard, mouse, printer, etc.) or computer program and interpret what it needs. It mainly comprises a computer chip that contains billions of small transistors. Every single calculation gets carried out within the given transistors. Like the motherboard, the CPU is essential to the functionality of the computer. Computers cannot function without one.

2.2.6 Mouse

The mouse, considered an input device, is a hand-held pointing device that detects two-dimensional motion relative to the screen. The mouse can be wired or wireless. The mouse utilizes a laser ball to scroll through the screen. Any given movement operated from the mouse sends direct information into the computer to move the cursor on the screen.

Figure 2.3 Examples of hardware.

2.2.7 Keyboard

The keyboard is a hardware component used to provide commands to the computer and input text. It can be wired or wireless. It comprises alphabets, special characters, numbers, and extra buttons to provide input into the computer. The keyboard is the input device used to take feedback from the user and process commands.

2.2.8 Printer

The printer is a component used to print something visible on a computer and transfer the information displayed to paper. Printers vary in cost, speed, size, and sophistication (Figure 2.3).

2.3 Hardware Dependence (Reliance)

Hardware starts functioning once the software is loaded. The hardware depends on software to operate. Hardware that has no set of programs (software) upon which to function is useless. For example, the computer is a piece of hardware that must have the relevant software loaded to carry out a specific task. Hardware is considered a one-time expense. In simple terms, hardware can be thought of as the heart of a computer system, while the software can be thought of as the computer system's soul.

2.4 Hardware Failure

It is important to note that almost all hardware will fail at some point. Hardware can fail for a plethora of reasons. Hardware can be physically sabotaged, break as a result of innocent misuse, or see its electrical efficiency diminish over time. And there are several other ways hardware can fail. Therefore, hardware failure is something that affects everyone. The loss of hardware needs to be repaired, or the offending part needs to be replaced. For example, individuals must worry that their cell phone battery is losing its charge. Companies create business continuity plans for when their servers go down due to natural disasters. Both companies and individuals need to consider that hard drives can fail at any given time, and the data will become corrupted.

2.5 Hardware Durability

The durability of hardware relates to the fact that it wears out as time passes. Due to the inevitability of hardware failure at some point, companies are continually seeking ways to improve their hardware durability. Lithium-ion batteries, for instance, are continuously being developed to hold a higher charge, degrade slower with use, and be more efficient in terms of physical size. Companies are also looking for alternatives besides lithium-ion batteries that are more efficient and can be produced at the same price or cheaper. There is a relative scale of durability for each aspect of hardware, and there are people always searching for ways to improve hardware (Table 2.1).

2.6 Chapter Summary

Hardware is the physical part of technology when compared to software. Most devices share the same internal components, with the components themselves varying in size and power. Hardware can be

Table 2.1 Hardware Explained

TERM	DESCRIPTION
Definition	Devices that are required to store and run (execute) the software
Types	Input, processing, storage, control, and output devices
Function	Delivery system for software solutions
Examples	Monitor, headphones, printer, scanners, routers, modems, projector, etc.
Interdependency	Starts to work (operate) once software is loaded
Failure	Failure is random
Durability	Wears out over time
Nature	Physical (visible) in nature

as small as a cell phone in your pocket or as large as a supercomputer that fills an entire room. Different hardware types serve different purposes, but external hardware devices and internal hardware devices are the two common types. Peripheral devices such as external disk drives, keyboards, and monitors are also considered as hardware. Equipment such as printers and scanners are used to capture data, transform it, and present it to the user as output. A major advantage of hardware is that people are usually more interested in buying hardware devices. Humanity would not have progressed as far as it has without developing better and faster hardware. Hardware will continue to be developed in more efficient and powerful ways.

Chapter Review Questions

Multiple Choice Questions

1. What are three examples of information technology hardware?
   A. Computer, laptop, iPad
   B. Printer, keyboard, mouse
   C. Server, router, cables
   D. All the above

True or False

2. Diagnostic tools are an example of an operating system.
   True
   False

3. Hubs and routers are examples of software.
   True
   False
4. RAM is not responsible for loading the operating system on the computer's boot.
   True
   False
5. RAM is volatile.
   True
   False
6. Hardware is wearable.
   True
   False

Fill in the Blanks

7. ________consists of everything in the physical layer of information technology.
8. ________is physical in nature.

3
Software

3.1 Introduction

Software is one of the major components of the technological aspect of any information system. To fully understand information technology, you will need to know how the software component works.

3.2 Software

Hardware must be told what to do. Software operates directly on hardware devices and tells (instructs) the hardware what to do as well as when and how to do it. Although the CPU of a computer consists of hardware that acts as the computer's brain, the CPU is useless without the software's instruction. In the previous chapter we introduced the analogy of bike riding to help explain hardware. Continuing with that analogy, we can see that the knowledge of how to ride the bike and where you want to go represents the software. The head has the information that instructs the body how to pedal and maneuver while also providing a destination. Without your brain, the bike is just a metal object that does not do anything.

Software plays a mediating role between the user and the computer hardware. In the absence of software, a user essentially cannot perform any task on a computer. This means that software encompasses all the data, applications, and programs stored electronically. A system can be created with the help of hardware. However, this system without any software will be nothing but a showpiece. To work efficiently, the system needs various kinds of software. The software will help the system run efficiently, protect it from viruses, or help navigate the Internet. Software may seem more expensive than hardware. However, when you buy software like Office 365 you get not only a product but also a continuing service. The service provided by such software becomes better with every update. Hence, the value of the software increases over time.

DOI: 10.1201/9781003204114-3

3.3 Types of Software

Software can be categorized into two types: operating system (system software) and application software.

3.3.1 Operating System

The operating system (OS) controls and manages the hardware and other software on the hardware. The OS is used to manage the computer hardware's behavior in order to offer basic functionalities to meet user needs. In other words, the OS acts as an intermediary between the user and the hardware.

To illustrate, let's use the example of a child's fire truck toy with lights and sound. The toy's inner part contains a digital circuit board (PCB board), mounted in external rubber buttons that can be pressed. The PCB board contains a basic micro-controller, read-only memory (ROM) chip, and wires that go to the lights and speakers. When the child presses the buttons (input), a signal triggers a circuit on the micro-controller that reads from random-access memory (RAM) and executes an instruction that plays sounds through the speakers and triggers the light (output). The board itself, in this scenario, acts as the operating system.

The operating system makes the hardware usable and operates directly on hardware devices (Figure 3.1). The operating system is almost always pre-installed on your device. Some examples of OS include Microsoft Windows on a personal computer and Google's Android on a mobile phone. Microsoft Windows operating system has introduced many different versions, including the most recent ones, Windows 10, Windows 8, Windows 7, and Windows Vista. Windows comes pre-loaded on most new personal computers, making it the most popular operating system. The Android App Store runs multiple apps simultaneously, making it easier for users to use software ranging from games to office applications without wandering throughout the Internet.

From the moment the user powers on the computer to the final moment before it shuts down, the OS plays a vital role in its functionality. The OS connects with the computer's CPU and various storage and memory. The operating system acts as a binding agent for software, hardware, and users.

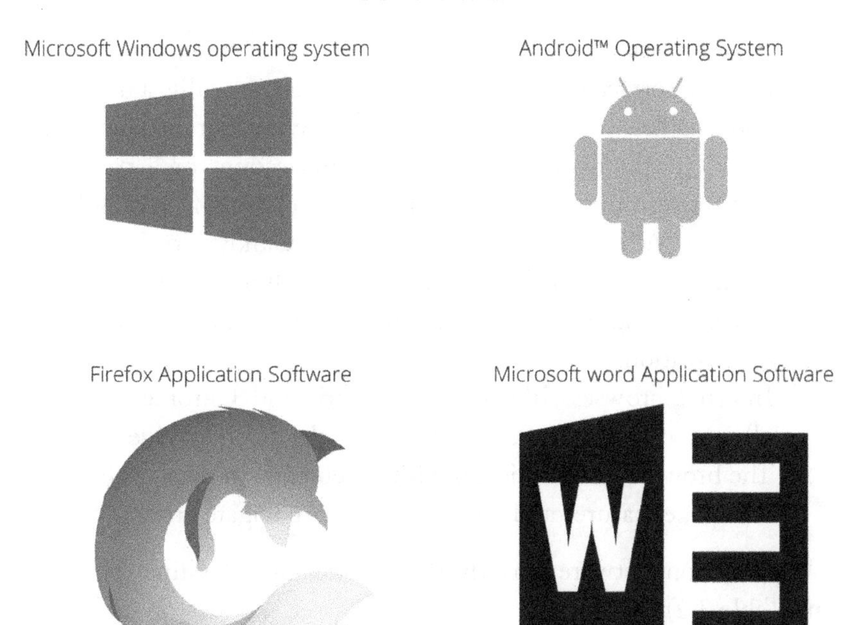

Figure 3.1 Software examples.

3.3.2 Application Software

Application software (*app* for short) is designed to benefit users to perform one or more tasks (see Figure 3.1). It is pretty much everything that is within your hardware. Examples of apps include the message board at the bus station that lets travelers know that their bus is delayed, the self-serve checkout at the supermarket, an ATM that tells customers their account balance, traffic lights that direct vehicles, and the weather forecast. More common application software programs include the following:

- Microsoft suite of products including Office, Excel, Word, PowerPoint, Outlook, and so on. Almost everybody has seen an Excel spreadsheet filled out with numbers. Word processing software allows you to enter text into the app and then edit it.
- Mobile apps that extend the productivity and reach of a business. Once a business or employee's mobile device is equipped with apps, business transactions can be performed in the

fastest possible time, such as while out of the office traveling, making service calls, during sales calls, etc. Usually, a mobile app enables you to do something specific. For instance, a banking app for accessing your bank account or a payroll app for running payroll. It also includes communication apps such as WhatsApp or games such as Candy Crush Saga. Other apps may include information such as about weather or transportation or apps enabling customers to interact with organizations.

- Internet browsers like Firefox, Safari, and Chrome. These allow the user to access and browse the World Wide Web. The browser communicates with a web page to display all the web page features and allow the user to navigate around it.

Application software can either be installed or run online (Table 3.1 and Table 3.2).

3.4 Chapter Summary

The need for information technology has increased rapidly, as most organizations today need IT to conduct business. Software instructs the hardware on what to do as well as when and how to do it.

Table 3.1 Basic Differences between Operating System and Application Software

KEY	OPERATING SYSTEM	APPLICATION SOFTWARE
Definition	Interface between application software and system	Runs as per user request on the platform which is provided by system software
Development Language	Developed in low-level language more compatible with the hardware	Developed in high-level language and developed as some specific purpose software
Usage	Used for operating hardware	Used to perform specific tasks
Installation	Installed on the hardware (computer)	Installed according to user's requirements
User interaction	Specific to system hardware; less or no user interaction is available in system software	Users can interact with it as the user interface is available
Dependency	Runs independently and provides a platform for running application software	Cannot run independently without the system software
Examples	Compiler, debugger, assembler, driver, etc.	Word processor, web browser, media player, etc.

Table 3.2 Software Explained

KEY	DESCRIPTION
Definition	Instructions that enable a user to interact with the hardware. Program that enables a device (hardware) to perform a specific task, as opposed to the hardware (physical components of the system).
Types	Application software and system software
Function	Helps to perform a specific task
Examples	Adobe Acrobat, QuickBooks, Google Chrome, Microsoft Excel, Microsoft Word
Interdependency	Installed on hardware in order to deliver its set of instructions
Failure	Failure is systematic
Durability	Does not wear out over time, but bugs are discovered in software as time passes
Nature	Logical in nature

Operating system (system software) and application software are the two categories of software. The operating system acts as an intermediary between the user and the hardware. The operating system makes the hardware usable and operates directly on hardware devices. Application software is basically everything that is within your hardware.

Some IT workers may spend more time configuring hardware components, but those components are also governed by software. An IT professional's role includes deploying and setting up software applications for users. Therefore, it is vital to know and understand these distinctions.

Chapter Review Questions

1. In one paragraph, explain how software impacts hardware. Give examples.
2. Give an example of IT software.
3. Microsoft Windows is an example of which component of IT?
4. What is application software?
5. What do you understand by software? Discuss its types.
6. Explain the difference between hardware and software with their definition and uses.
7. Why operating system is the most important type of system software?
8. What are the functions of the operating system?

9. From the list, distinguish between operating systems and applications: Microsoft Excel, Google Chrome, iTunes, Windows, Android, Angry Birds.
10. What is your favorite software application? What tasks does it help you accomplish?

Multiple Choice Questions

11. Which of the following is not an example of application software?
    A. Candy Crush
    B. Microsoft Access Database
    C. Google Docs
    D. Android
12. Which of the following is an example of an operating system?
    A. Hardware
    B. Unix
    C. Media player
    D. Outlook
13. Which of these are examples of application software? Select all that apply.
    A. Office
    B. Android
    C. Skype
    D. Firefox
14. Which of the following is not an operating system?
    A. Mac
    B. DOS
    C. P
    D. Linux
15. The instructions that tell the computer what to do and how to do it are called:
    A. Software
    B. Hardware
    C. Mouse
    D. Printer
    E. Monitor

16. ________ are almost always pre-installed on a device
    A. Operating systems
    B. Desktop
    C. Software
    D. Computer

Fill in the Blanks

17. ________ is the set of coded instruction that brings the machinery to life.
18. Software is often divided into two major categories, namely ________ and ________, which make the computer run.
19. The most important type of system software is ________ because it provides the user with the interface to communicate with the hardware and other software on the computer and manages system resources.
20. ________manages the hardware components, including a single workstation of a global network with many clients.
21. ________consists of programs that support day-to-day business functions and provide users with the information they need.
22. ________consists of everything in the physical layer of information technology.
23. ________refers to the programs that control the hardware and produce the desired information or results.
24. ________are almost always pre-installed on a device.
25. ________enables a device to perform a specific task.
26. ________is logical in nature.

4
Communication Network

4.1 Introduction

Networks, connections, and relationships drive human survival and growth through interaction and innovation. No matter how new they seem, innovations and inventions have always depended on expanding and adapting previously established ideas. Take electricity for an example. If not for Homo erectus discovering fire millions of years ago, there would have been no basis for the concepts leading to the discovery of electricity. Fire discovery led to using candles and light to use at night during the dark. This, in turn, led to the ideas enabling the utilization of electricity. Light has been a significant phase of humanity.

Additionally, the need for trade in order to exchange goods and services has over the years led to the growth of certain technologies for improving how we conduct business. The use of barter trade was challenging because traders would exchange more valuable goods for less valuable goods. This led to the invention of paper money, enabling people to conduct trade, grow the economy, and create opportunities for success. These inventions and innovations would have been incomplete without the help of networking.

Networking is the process by which people relate to each other to share information regarding common interests and beliefs. The computer system has been modeled and developed in relation to the real world. It embodies most of the tasks and processes of our daily activities. This includes the way we relate and share information with each other to enable decision-making. Hence, computer networks refer to the way computer systems and computer devices are connected and communicate with each other for the purpose of sharing information.

DOI: 10.1201/9781003204114-4

4.2 Computer Networks

Networks are basically connections between multiple hardware devices. A network enables all components within a system to connect and function as one unit. A computer network is a collection of two or more computers connected to share information and resources. A network can be as small as two computers or as large as millions of devices. The keyword in the definition is *sharing*—this is the main purpose of computer networking. The ability to share information efficiently is what gives computer networking its power and appeal.

Envision a network as a project team. Through the efforts of all involved—the sharing of time, talent, and resources—a goal is accomplished or a project is completed. Personal computers are powerful tools that can quickly process and manipulate large amounts of data, but they do not allow users to share these data efficiently. Before networks, users needed to either print documents or copy files to a disk for others to edit or use them. If others made changes to the documents or files, there was no easy way to merge the changes. This is known as a *stand-alone environment.* However, when two computers are linked together using a cable that allows them to share data, it is known as a *networked environment.*

Technological advances in networking hardware and software have led to greater throughput on all scales and increasingly tighter integration of networking across all computing aspects. In tandem with these advances, the idea of networking has entered the common consciousness to an extent that would have been unimaginable a few years ago. This shift in perception has led to an expansion of networking beyond the workplace, which is already beginning to shape developments in networking technology.

An example of computer networks is the use of the Internet. When connected to the Internet, that connection is established as long as the name is valid and regardless of the user's location or time of access. For example, suppose a user wants to access CNN's website. The user logs in to their web browser and ensures there is an internet connection. Next, the user proceeds to enter the name of the site they want to access. In this case, the site is *cnn.com.* After entering, the computer sends a query to the host computer, and data are returned. All of this happens in a matter of seconds. The host computer returns the information in a format that allows the user to view the site's texts and graphics and enables the user to click on links.

A computer network system comprises a series of devices including computers, routers, switches, servers, and much more. These devices have a series of connections that make them work to communicate with one another. Again using our bike riding example from Chapter 3, the chain, pedals, wheels, and handlebars make up the bike network. These are a series of connections that enable the bike to work. They depend on each other to work correctly. The pedals and the chain move the wheels, the body and the handlebars steer to provide the motive force and fine-tuning for navigation.

4.2.1 Hardware Aspects of Networks

A network hardware component consists of physical devices. Hardware is what makes a system work. Without hardware, a system cannot function properly. Without the mouse, keyboard, or CPU, for example, a computer will not function properly. Network hardware uses cables to connect the various devices and junction boxes like the one in Figure 4.1.

In Figure 4.1, the computers serve as the workstation, i.e., the place where work gets done. The switch provides a central connection point for cable from the workstation. The repeater and switch connect network devices so that they can function as a single segment. As you see in the figure, the repeater and the switch connect the workstation to the system so they can function as one unit. The router connects and transfers data packets out of and into the network. The bridge in this

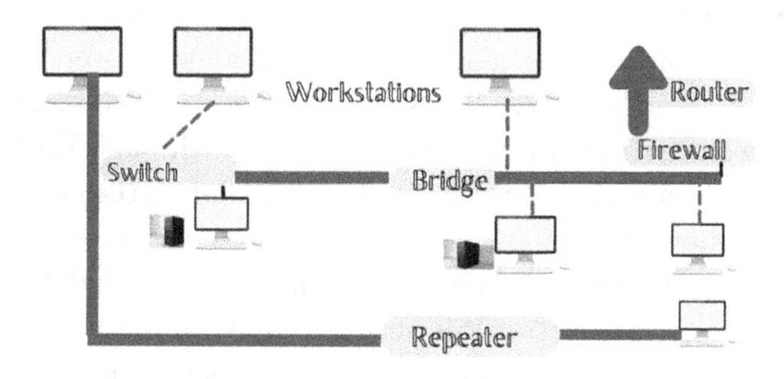

Figure 4.1 Basic network (hardware).

figure connects two Ethernet network segments and forwards packets from the source network to the destined network.

4.2.2 Software Aspects of Networks

Unlike hardware, software does not have any physical components but consists of programs that run on the hardware. To create a network, software also is required. Software functions include testing a network, monitoring and controlling a network, and securing a network from intrusions and malware. For example, the firewall component in Figure 4.1 helps protect the network by blocking unauthorized access to the system. In other words, the firewall can be thought of as the gatekeeper of the network.

The software has linked protocols that allow a set of hardware networks that can be used. The protocols defined are standard and followed by everyone who needs to set up a network. The software is the driving force that instructs all network components to operate together.

4.3 Types of Networks

While many types of networks exist, the two main categories are Local Area Network (LAN) and Wide Area Network (WAN). Let's consider these in turn.

4.3.1 Local Area Network

A Local Area Network (LAN) connects a small number of computer systems in a relatively close geographical area. In other words, a LAN is limited to a specific location, such as a home, office, or building. A single router may be used in a home network to offer connections. For example, a hardware (computer) may connect to the router via Ethernet, while smartphones connect through Wi-Fi. All connected devices share the same network and often the same internet connection. A more extensive network, such as an educational institution's network, may comprise many switches and Ethernet cables. This type of network is still considered a LAN because of its limited specificity. The nodes are independent but are all connected via the LAN. Switches and routers are part of the devices that allow a LAN device to interconnect them with each other. In a LAN, connected computers have a Network Operating System (NOS) installed onto them.

One computer is designated as the file server that stores all the software controlling the network. It also stores the software that can be shared by the computers attached to the network. Other computers connected to the file server are called workstations. The workstations can be less powerful than the file server, and they may have additional software on their hard drives. LANs allow computers to share resources, access each other's data files, and even control one computer via another. LAN has been the driving force of Internet of Things technology. Also, the invention and growth of Ethernet connection and wireless connection have highly increased and influenced LAN used by most industries and organizations. On most LANs, cables are used to connect the computers. Generally, LAN offers a bandwidth of 10–100 Mbps. LAN has a higher data speed and transfer rate but is limited with the LAN's reach or coverage.

4.3.2 Wide Area Network

A Wide Area Network (WAN) is not limited to a single area but spans across a large geographic area, such as a state, province, or country. WAN connects more than one LAN over a considerable geographic distance. These kinds of networks connect using telephone lines, satellite links, and other long-range communications technologies. Customers can use WAN to communicate with other users, regardless of their location, provided they are using the same established WAN. Such networks are designed to serve hundreds or thousands of miles, such as public and private packet switching networks and national telephone networks. For example, a company with offices in New York, Virginia, and California may connect through a WAN. WANs often consist of multiple LANs that are connected over the Internet. Access to WANs may be limited using firewalls, authentication, and other security measures.

Without WAN connections, organizations would be restricted to a particular location or specific geographic region. LANs would only allow organizations to work within their building. However, growth to outside areas—whether in different cities or countries—would be impossible. As business organizations become international, WANs allow them to communicate between branches and stay connected. With WANs, students at universities may be able to access library databases or university research. People rely every day on WANs to communicate, bank, shop, and more.

The network software helps administrators deploy, manage, and monitor the network and allows the hardware (devices/computers) to share, send, and receive data files via the network. Some of WAN's advantages are that it allows connectivity of different devices and allows connectivity of devices connected in far geographical areas. Communication between branch offices can be improved using e-mail and file sharing. It facilitates a centralized company-wide data backup system. Companies located in various small, interrelated offices can store files centrally and access each other's information.

However, WANs are not without their challenges. Due to the high number of interconnected devices, the network is liable to attacks. If a failure does occur, it might take longer for a technician to resolve the issue because of the high number of connected devices. Additionally, a WAN setup is costly, and a technician will be needed on a continuing basis.

4.4 Network Operating System

A network operating system is an operating system used to support network resources and ensure that computers communicate efficiently and effectively. The primary purpose of a network operating system is to ensure that a computer resource's hardware components work efficiently and effectively as needed. For example, in an organization where the computers are connected and use a shared printer, each connected computer must print no matter the length and size of what is being printed from it. The network operating system also facilitates the use and interconnecting of devices and systems by ensuring that security is maintained.

Networks are very vulnerable to attacks and must be protected against hackers. When hackers gain access to an organization's private and protected information, it leads to severe consequences. Such a breach may lead to the loss of customers and clients because of a lack of trust. Additionally, such an attack would result in financial losses and the information that was stolen could land in competitors' hands.

Computer networking is critical in any organization to ensure interoperability. For example, if the finance department did not have a way to share resources and information with the marketing department, then the marketing department would be hampered by this lack of information and unable to improve marketing tactics. The two major network operating systems are client–server networks and peer-to-peer networks.

4.4.1 Client–Server Network

The client–server network is made up of two words, i.e., *client* and *server*. The idea is that in this network, each computer is either a client or a server. A centralized host computer is identified as the server, and a user's individual workstation is identified as the client for complete a particular task. In other words, the client refers to either the hardware components of the computer or software responsible for accessing services being offered by the server. On the other end, a server is a system responsible for allowing computer devices to access certain services provided on a network. The client requests a service from the server, and the server responds by providing that service.

A typical example of a client–server network is sending an e-mail. First, the e-mail is transmitted to the source server. Next, the e-mail is transmitted to the destination server. Lastly, the destination server sends the e-mail to the client at the other end. Servers are responsible for transmitting the message, while the client is responsible for sending and receiving the message.

4.4.2 Functions of the Client–Server Network

A network is also responsible for ensuring that it provides feedback regardless of how many computers request access to resources. As stated earlier, a computer network is also responsible for ensuring that security is maintained when a computer is accessing resources or certain information on the network. The client–server network's responsibility is to control access to all the resources and information. In other words, it is the responsibility of the client–server network to ensure that there is an established, safe, and secure internet connection. Suppose an organization shares several applications across different departments. In that case, it is the client–server network's responsibility to maintain the shared applications and allow easy access to those applications.

The client–server network manages the traffic flow and ensures that services are executed as needed. Since the client–server network is also used as a data storage center, it is also used for backup. If a user wants to access the backup, the server allows access. In terms of access, it stores passwords and user accounts and makes access to resources based on the level of access. A client–server network is like a community center where people all come together to play, share information, shop, and engage in other numerous services. It is the responsibility of the client–server network to ensure this happens. A client–server network is one of the most popular and preferred networks because of the numerous benefits that it offers.

4.4.3 Advantages and Disadvantages

Apart from security, the network offers several benefits to its users. One important benefit is that of the server being resistant to failure in the event that one of the client computers malfunctions. The malfunction of one client computer does not affect the server. Another advantage is due to its centralized nature that allows for easy access to resources. Employees or users can access resources easily as well as sharing them. Yet another advantage is increased processing speeds among client computers. Since the client computer serves only one role, the computers perform their functions efficiently. Consequently, it allows for better security measures because of its centralized nature. There is easy administration, and the network can be expanded.

Drawbacks of a client–server network are that the server network's failure will lead to client computers' failure. Server networks are expensive to implement and maintain. Furthermore, they require specialized knowledge and a constant need for technicians to assist in their maintenance.

4.4.4 Peer-to-Peer Networks

Peer-to-peer (P2P) networks are types of networks in which each computer has its own memory and resources and can handle an equal number of tasks as the next computer. In other words, a P2P network does not rely on dedicated servers for communication. Instead, it uses direct connections between clients (peers). In this network, every node can perform its own functions. The computers are connected through these nodes. One single computer can decide to share its resources with other computers on the node. However, the connection will only occur via what is known as a *hub* or a *switch*.

The network operating system is responsible for ensuring that nodes can communicate with each other and allow connections. Since the nodes are independent, a node can decide to allow or initiate communication with a remote node. The connection is allowed only if the authentication is permitted by the network operating system. P2P networks are directly connected, and any computer (or any node) has the responsibility of being either a server or a client. The differentiation between the server and the client depends on the type of service. If the node is offering a service, it acts as a server. When requesting a service, it acts as a client. P2P networks can take either a wired or a wireless connection.

4.4.5 Advantages and Disadvantages

One of the main advantages of a P2P network is that it is cost-effective to implement and maintain. Additionally, P2P networks are very easy to implement. No special skills and knowledge are required to set up such a network. Furthermore, the failure of one node cannot affect the functionality of other nodes on the network.

A disadvantage of P2P networks is that they are not highly secure. Due to their independent nature, it is easy for unauthorized personnel to access any network node. Additionally, they do not require any access permission. Their decentralization does not need data storage to be managed and maintained efficiently. Furthermore, it is hard to achieve data backup because of the decentralized nature of the network.

4.5 Network Devices

Networking devices are simply hardware devices that expand the reach, search, and access of a network. In other words, network devices are the physical devices required for communication and interaction between hardware on a network. They can be used to connect computers, fax machines, printers, and other electronic devices to a network. The functionalities of network devices have been transformed and segregated based on the task handled by the device (Table 4.1).

Table 4.1 Network Devices

DEVICES	DESCRIPTION
Hub	• Connects multiple computer networking devices • Basic element that extends the network range and broadcasts the same signal to the rest of the ports • Does not filter data but instead retransmits incoming data packets or frames to all parts
Router	• Connectivity device used to connect two LANs • Responsible for transmitting data in the form of data packets between LANs • Filters and forwards data based on a logical address
Modem	• Responsible for establishing a connection to send and receive data over telephone or cable line • Converts digital signals into analog and vice versa to enable data transfer
Network Interface Card (NIC)	• Allows the computer to connect and interact with other Local Area Network devices • Comes installed as a hardware component
Switch	• Generally, involves a more intelligent role than hubs • Connects other Ethernet devices • Contains the addresses of data packets allowing it to send data packets to their correct address • Responsible for storing data packets on the network • Responsible for error checking on the data packets • Improves network efficiency over routers or hubs because of the virtual circuit capability
Gateway	• Connects two or more networks that use different protocols
Bridge	• A kind of network device which sits between two different LANs • Joins multiple LANs so as to be able to communicate with each other • Used to open communications among different departments within a corporation or among different corporations who have shared services and trust certificates that are current and valid
Access Points	• Act as a terminal to provide (mostly wireless) network access • Mounted on a clear and elevated position in an office setting to minimize echoes and interference • Transmit services for registered devices via radio frequencies

4.5.1 Network Topologies

A network topology refers to how the devices in a network are arranged to allow communication between the devices. Recall that a network consists of several communication devices, hardware, and software connected through a link. A link in a network refers to a communication path between two or more devices. The communication process can be achieved with the help of network topology. In other words, the network topology is the geometrical representation of links and nodes.

The two types of topologies are physical and logical. The *physical topology* is the actual physical arrangement of the network's devices that describes how nodes are connected. The physical connection can be made using wires, wireless connectivity, networking components, and more. *Logical topology* is a high-level representation of how two or more nodes are connected. In simplified terms, it is the way in which the devices communicate internally.

There are several different physical and logical network topologies from which administrators can choose to build a secure and easily maintainable topology. The following is a summary of the most common types of topologies.

Bus Topology. Bus topology is a local network type in which workstations (nodes) are connected to a single cable and data flow is one way. When a sender sends a message, all nodes hear it but it only gets delivered to the intended receiver that accepts it while others reject it.

Advantages of bus topology include low cost and easy installation process. Disadvantages include that the failure of the shared communication channel leads to failure of all the devices, that the communication flow is uni-directional, that loss of packets would be final, and that if the integrity of the cable is compromised, the network itself is compromised.

Ring Topology. In ring topology all the nodes are connected in a circle or closed loop, i.e., the computers are connected in the form of a ring. Each node has two neighbors. This means that every computer is connected to two other computers. Computers can connect to computers that are adjacent or next to each other. However, for a computer to send data to a computer that is not adjacent to it, data must go through each computer until it reaches its destination.

The advantages of using ring topology are that it can handle high traffic volume, and there is equal access to resources by all the computers. However, one of this topology's disadvantages is that data must pass every single node before reaching its destination.

Star Topology. In a star topology devices are connected in the form of a star. All the devices are connected to a central hub and every device connects directly to that hub. The hub might be a router, bridge, or even a gateway. Communication to each device is secure and private. Data losses are minimal. If one link fails, the integrity of the network remains. Additional nodes could be added to the network or discounted from the network without any discrepancies.

This topology's disadvantage is its cost to install as this topology would require a dedicated line from each node. Additionally, if the centralized hub is down, the entire network is down, and each device would behave as a stand-alone device.

Tree Topology. In this topology the devices are connected in a branched-out style. Secondary hubs supervise each branch. This is one of the successful topologies which has its applications in WAN and some LAN settings. Tree topology is one of the most common topologies used by most networks.

Some of the advantages of this topology involve the fact that it has a centralized framework. Hence, the connection is very flexible. If the root node fails for some reason, it will not bring down the entire grid; the secondary nodes will continue to operate. However, the topology faces several challenges in that once there is a failure, the entire network fails.

Mesh Topology. Mesh topology is a type of topology where computers are interconnected to each other, i.e., all the nodes are interconnected as in point-to-point. This means that one node may be connected to all the other nodes or just a few in the entire network. Every node must be connected to every other active node that belongs to the network. Setting up such a network is labor intensive because of cable usage that translates to more capital investment for procuring its hardware portion. One of the advantages of mesh topology is that there is a better connection of devices minimizing connection failures. Additionally, a configuration of the topology is easy. However, it is costly to implement and maintain.

Hybrid Topology. Hybrid topology is a combination of two or more recognized topologies linked together. In other words, a hybrid is an interconnection of two or more basic network topologies, each of which contains its own nodes. A hybrid topology can include a mix of mesh, bus, ring, star, and tree topologies. These kinds of hybrid topologies are commonly found in companies where each team has its own special networking requirements.

A network layout has a direct impact on its functionality. Selecting the right topology can improve performance and data efficiency and reduce operational and maintenance costs such as cabling costs. Network topology is important because it plays a significant role in the functioning of networks, helps administrators better understand the networking concepts, and helps reduce the operational costs.

4.5.2 Open System Interconnection

The Open System Interconnection (OSI) network management model is the standard model and provides a conceptual framework for organizing a diverse range of network resources. The OSI model involves seven layers through which secure communications can be accomplished over the network to the intended recipient. Each layer performs a specific task. Without any of the layers there will not be a successful handshake. Here are the seven layers and a brief description of each (Table 4.2).

4.6 Chapter Summary

A network is basically a connection between multiple hardware devices that enable file or resource sharing as well as protection of data in any network system. Networks are made up of hardware and software. Successful business requires a combination of correct hardware, software, and a speedy network. While many types of networks exist, the two primary categories are LAN and WAN. LAN is limited to a specific location, such as a home, office, or building. A single router may be used in a home network to offer connections. On the other hand, WAN connects more than one LAN over a considerable geographic distance.

A network operating system ensures that a computer resource's hardware components work efficiently and effectively as needed. The two major network operating systems are client–server networks and Peer-to-Peer (P2P) networks. Client–server networks are designed

Table 4.2 Seven Layers of the OSI Model

#	LAYER	DESCRIPTION
7	Application	The interface gives the user and the software a chance to interact with each other, allowing for the connection and communication of software with the user.
6	Presentation	The presentation layer is responsible for presenting data that have already been processed in a format that the user can understand. This layer defines how the packet should be encoded or encrypted so that the recipient can translate it to its intended form.
5	Session	This layer is responsible for the connection or communication between different computers. It is responsible for ensuring the correct authentication processes are followed.
4	Transport	The transport layer is responsible for transmitting data packets between the network systems. It is responsible for making sure the physical cables can carry the packets without any echoes, data losses, and attenuation. This layer reads if the packet was successfully received at the other end. If not, it sends feedback to resend that particular package.
3	Network	The network layer is responsible for transferring data to its destination. It uses the logical framework and obtains each data packet's address to ensure it reaches its destination. Every package contains an address, i.e., an IP address.
2	Datalink	This layer is responsible for ensuring the flow of data from one node to another.
1	Physical	This layer is the lowest layer of the model and deals with the physical attributes of the network. It is involved with transmitting the data that are inputted into the device. It is responsible for transmitting raw data from the input device into the receiving device. It converts data into bytes and bits.

for clients (end-users) to access files or other services from a server (central computer). A server's sole purpose is to serve its clients. P2P networks are those in which each computer has its own memory and resources and can handle the number of equal tasks as the next computer.

Network devices are the physical devices required for communication and interaction between hardware on a network. They connect computers, fax machines, printers, and other electronic devices to a network. Network topology refers to how the devices in a network are arranged to allow communication between the devices. The two types of topologies are physical and logical. The physical topology describes how nodes are physically connected. Logical topology is the way in which the devices communicate internally. Common types of topologies include bus, ring, star, tree, mesh, and hybrid.

The Open System Interconnection provides a conceptual framework for organizing a diverse range of network resources and has seven layers that communicate securely over the network to the intended recipient. Each layer performs a specific task.

Chapter Review Questions

1. What is a network? In a paragraph, explain your understanding of a network.
2. In your own words, give an example of network.
3. What is the difference between Local Area Network and Wide Area Network? Give examples.
4. What is a network operating system?
5. What is a network topology?
6. What are two advantages of client–server network?
7. What are two disadvantages of peer-to-peer networks?
8. Name the 7 OSI.

Multiple Choice Questions

9. Connections between multiple devices
   A. Hardware
   B. Network
   C. Software
   D. Application software
10. ________can be thought of as the gatekeeper of the network.
    A. Router
    B. Firewall
    C. Repeater
    D. Network
11. ________is the driving force that instructs all network components to operate together.
    A. Hardware
    B. Network
    C. Software
    D. None

12. The two primary categories of network are
    A. LEN and WAN
    B. LAN and WAN
    C. LEN and WEN
    D. None

True or False

13. Network is made up of only software.
    True
    False
14. Network can be as small as two computers only.
    True
    False
15. Repeater and switch connect network devices so that they can function as different segments.
    True
    False
16. Router connects and transfers data packets out of and into the network.
    True
    False
17. To create a network, software is also required.
    True
    False
18. LAN is limited to a specific location.
    True
    False

Fill in the Blanks

19. ________ connect multiple hardware devices.
20. ________ is limited to a specific location.

5

Careers in Information Technology

5.1 Introduction

Not all students research the field of information technology before pursuing a career in it. And many students fail to pursue an IT career on account of their limited (and sometimes complete lack of) knowledge about the field. This chapter is purposely designed for students in this position. The chapter describes various topics that extend students' interest and looks at the requirements to help gauge suitability for pursuing an IT career.

5.2 Are You a Fit for an IT Career?

You might be wondering whether an IT career is the right fit for you! In fact, anyone can study IT; however, individuals who aspire to enter the field should develop a solid basis in logic and critical thinking skills. You should possess the abilities to listen, communicate, and maintain a professional attitude when faced with frustrating problems. You should envision the issues at hand and find potential solutions as quickly as possible for the sake of business continuity.

Consider, for instance, the sort of critical and creative thinking involved in being an IT help desk technician. One issue in this job is learning to understand and interpret the customer's technical abilities, as what they say or ask is not always what they mean. The customer may have reported *their computer does not work*. But this could mean many things! Figuring out even the basis to begin providing service can be a complicated process.

In another instance, if a customer complains that their cursor is not responsive (i.e., they are not able to move it around on the screen), this could be an indication of a locked-up computer, or an unplugged USB mouse, or even a malware issue. IT professionals sometimes

DOI: 10.1201/9781003204114-5

encounter users who confuse an internet browser window with network connectivity. Managing these users requires IT professionals to put themselves in the customer's shoes. This means reverse-engineering the customer's thought processes, figuring out the true problem, and then communicating the best solution.

One's passion for technology as well as a positive attitude can help them succeed and advance their IT career pursuit. Combining these traits fosters a greater potential for success.

5.3 Education and Degrees

Information technology is a rapidly growing field that offers several positions for its professionals. Students with solid technical skills and an aptitude for gathering information and interpreting data are likely to succeed in this industry. Like most fields, disciplines in information technology are categorized ranging from certificate, to diploma, to degree. Let's consider each of these in turn.

5.3.1 Information Technology Certification

Usually, certification programs in information technology last no more than 12 months. These programs help students learn the basics of IT. These programs are often intended for students who want to be exposed to a broad understanding of IT concepts and principles. Coursework completed in an IT certification program might later be transferable to a higher-level (i.e., associate or bachelor's) IT degree program. IT certificate holders may seek employment as help desk support technicians, network support technicians, or data center technicians.

5.3.2 Associate Degrees in IT

A typical associate degree program in information technology takes no more than two years to complete and includes a broad overview of IT along with general education courses. A high school diploma is typically required to enroll in an associate degree program in IT.

A graduate with an associate degree in IT may look for an entry-level job or transfer into a bachelor's degree program.

An associate degree program could require introductory coursework in computer networks, problem-solving, troubleshooting for computers, programming principles, and virtual communication strategies. Jobs could include an IT help desk associate, new business development associate, software engineer associate, or associate security consultant.

5.3.3 Bachelor's Degrees in Information Technology

A bachelor's degree in information technology usually requires four years to complete. The first two years often consist of introductory information technology courses and general education requirements. The last two years focus on the more specific and advanced aspects of the field.

While you may transfer credits from an associate degree toward a bachelor's IT program, you also can seek admission directly into a bachelor's program. With a bachelor's degree, you can explore the curriculum in greater depth and be able to specialize too. You can learn the fundamentals of IT operations, develop critical thinking skills, and determine what existing and new technologies can be deployed on a small or large scale.

In terms of employment opportunities, you can consider working as an IT analyst, IT support specialist, information systems manager, or systems administrator. Several companies, including Amazon, hire computer and IT employees in various fields ranging from program coordinators to risk specialists.

5.3.4 Master's Degrees in Information Technology

Unlike the bachelor's degree programs, master's degree programs in information technology dive deeper into the field's specialized and higher-level areas. Typically, a bachelor's degree is considered a prerequisite for admission to a master's program, as it lays the groundwork of essential skills and knowledge for the master's degree program. A master's degree program provides the opportunity to specialize.

This information technology degree can help you develop collaborative, communications, and real-world technical skills. With a master's degree in information technology, you might find employment as a manager of information technology operations, business systems manager, or information technology vice president. Of course, job titles vary from company to company and industry to industry.

5.3.5 Doctoral Degrees in Information Technology

Students who pursue a doctorate in information technology aim for a career in IT research or IT-based postsecondary education. A PhD is more focused on research, and doctoral programs are applicable to leadership and decision-making.

Doctoral degree programs allow students to learn more about their specialty and typically involve completing a dissertation. With a PhD in information technology, you can learn how to plan and report on research, deliver instruction at the college level, and design and evaluate information systems.

IT jobs for graduates with PhDs may include postdoctoral researcher, senior data scientist, or information technology president. Also, a computer research scientist position will likely require students to hold a doctoral degree. While doctoral graduates often find employment at universities, other employment options may include consulting, management, or government careers.

5.3.6 Continuing Education

Industries are constantly changing. Continuing education is designed for IT professionals to stay current with the latest developments, skills, and new technologies required in the field. Although continuing education is not always a requirement in information technology, many employers promote it. Your new knowledge also makes you more qualified for advanced work and an ideal candidate for promotions.

The information technology field comes with many certifications, which help IT professionals stay current. Some of these professional certifications may include the Oracle Certified Associate, Certified Information Systems Security Professional (CISSP), CompTIA's A+ Certifications, Project management professional (PMP), Certified ethical hacker (CEH), and Information Technology Infrastructure Library Foundation (ITIL).

These professional certifications can enhance IT careers and offer a wider choice to IT professionals. The courses involved help the professionals acquire in-depth knowledge and understanding of various programs and technologies as well as decide what field they would like to pursue. IT professionals can provide solutions to organizations including project management, which consists of defining, developing, arranging, and supervising various tasks related to the organization.

5.4 IT Fields

IT fields refer to higher education disciplines where students study toward a recognized certificate, diploma, or degree. The following sections explain how IT fields are defined in terms of academic disciplines.

5.4.1 Computer Engineering

Computer Engineering (CE) is a specialized technical domain IT field of study. Students are taught how to design and develop computer hardware, such as laptops, personal computers (PC), tablets, and other computer hardware components.

5.4.2 Management Information Systems

Management Information Systems (MIS) is a higher education information technology field of study that offers a non-technical business degree. Students in MIS study both business and management to understand how individuals and companies use data to inform and improve the decision-making process. Courses offered in this degree program may include database design, programming, and data analysis. However, the coursework mainly focuses on business-related topics, including finance, marketing, management principles, accounting, project management, leadership, and customer service.

5.4.3 Computer Information Systems

Computer Information Systems (CIS) prepares graduates for applying technology to business. In other words, CIS enables graduates to establish themselves in the workplace. A few of the IT jobs applicable to CIS are systems administrators, network administrators, database administrators, computer technicians, and computing security specialists.

Both MIS and CIS degrees help organizations manage people and processes through data and software. Jobs in these disciplines require professionals to have robust problem-solving, data analysis, and computer science skills.

The differences between MIS and CIS degrees are essential to know. These include the coursework students can expect to complete, industry-specific objectives, and the typical career paths for graduates in each program.

5.5 Careers in IT

The IT industry has opened many career paths to those willing to spend the time it takes to get a good education and technical training. Though most of these careers pay well, some of them are more stressful than others. Education level requirements differ among the different paths, but most require a four-year degree at a minimum. More technically complex jobs may need certifications in addition to a college degree. Table 5.1 presents a few different types of IT job titles, including their typical duties and minimum education requirements.

Keep in mind that some of these roles will change depending on the company's size and scope. IT professionals in smaller companies may be required to be a "Jack of all trades" with broader knowledge. Daily work may involve simple tasks like troubleshooting printers or more complex functions like employing specialized software to organize and keep track of data. On the other hand, IT employees have a more diverse array of potential focus areas within large firms. Some may work their way into management roles and others may pursue specialized areas like cybersecurity.

5.6 Projection of IT Career Growth

Careers in information technology are high paying, and the outlook for job growth is tremendous for many years to come. Occupations in information technology are expected to increase due to the role that information technology plays in our daily lives. Due to its importance

Table 5.1 IT Job Summaries

TITLE	JOB SUMMARY	MINIMUM EDUCATION
Computer Support Specialist	• Solves basic problems related to computer hardware and networks • Works on the front lines troubleshooting technical issues	Certificate
Computer Network Architect	• Designs and builds data communication networks	Bachelor's degree
Database Administrator	• Employs specialized software to organize and keep track of data • Diagnoses and solves complex IT issues related to data infrastructure • Ensures that an organization's data are safe, accessible, and easy to navigate	Bachelor's degree
IT Director	• Oversees the strategy and execution of IT operations for an organization • Ensures that department tasks align with company goals and development	Graduate degree
Network Systems Administrator	• Focuses on the big picture of the network system, security, and performance	Bachelor's degree
Computer Systems Analyst	• Works behind the scenes to marry IT with smart business solutions • Specializes in a particular industry while working for a technology firm or works directly in an industry, such as finance or government	Bachelor's degree
Information Security Analyst	• Responsible for the security of an organization's computer networks • Conducts tests and develops company-wide security best practices	Bachelor's degree
Programmer	• Creates the code for software applications and operating systems • Writes code that converts software developer designs into a set of instructions for a computer to follow	Bachelor's degree
Web Designer	• Constructs the overall look and feel of websites using images, CSS, HTML, JavaScript, etc. • Applies creative skills, such as for picking aesthetically pleasing color palettes	Associate degree
Quality Assurance Tester	• Checks software products to see if they're up to industry standards and free of any issues • Applies excellent time management and communication skills to help document test cases	Bachelor's degree
Professor	• Teaches both undergraduate and graduate courses	PhD
Instructor	• Teaches only undergraduate courses	Graduate degree
Chief Technology Officer	• Manages an organization's research and development as well as its technological needs	Graduate degree
Chief Information Officer	• Helps set and lead the technology strategy for an organization	Graduate degree

in industries and its high-paying nature, information technology is quickly becoming one of the fields that are in great demand. As the IT industry evolves to meet today's technology demands, different challenges are arising, and IT professionals are striving to meet them. IT professionals are responsible for helping individuals and organizations get their work done efficiently.

5.7 Further Considerations

Although IT offers a wide range of high-paying jobs, you as an individual must decide what interests you most before beginning your career journey in the field. If you do not find technology exciting, you could end up hating your job regardless of the compensation. Given the diversity of IT, on the other hand, the good news is that you can work toward an IT career that builds on your skills and interests by blending in other business knowledge.

5.8 Chapter Summary

Anyone can study information technology, but to succeed you should possess the abilities to listen, communicate, and maintain a professional attitude when faced with frustrating problems. Before pursuing a career in IT, you must first research the field. In other words, do not pursue a career in IT without doing your research and speaking with IT experts about their experience. Remember, experiences may differ from expert to expert. Like most fields, disciplines in information technology are categorized from certificate, to diploma, to degree. Careers in information technology are high paying, and the outlook for job growth is tremendous for many years to come. Occupations in information technology are expected to increase due to the role that information technology plays in our daily lives. We need people to continue studying the field in order to continue advancing IT.

Chapter Review Questions

1. What non-technical skills should an IT person have?
2. Why is it important to earn a four-year accredited IT degree if you want to work in the IT field?

3. What are some of the skills necessary to be an IT professional?
4. Why do help desk and computer technician careers require less education than other IT areas?
5. What are some of the various forms of continuing education available to an IT professional?
6. Name at least two IT-related careers that would not necessarily require a four-year degree.
7. Name three IT job titles.
8. Are you fit to pursue a career in information technology? Why and why not?
9. Continuing education is one of the most critical aspects of keeping up with IT's continual evolution. Explain how you hope to continue your education.

Multiple Choice Questions

10. You need a graduate degree in IT to teach all, except
    A. Associate degree in IT
    B. A certificate program in IT
    C. Bachelor's degree in IT
    D. PhD in IT
11. All are careers in IT, except
    A. Programmer
    B. Computer Analyst
    C. Meteorologist
    D. Network Administrator
12. ________ offers a non-technical IT degree
    A. Computer Engineer (CE)
    B. Management Information System (MIS)
    C. Computer Information System (CIS)
    D. All the above
13. ________ offers a technical IT degree
    A. Computer Information System (CIS)
    B. Computer Engineer (CE)
    C. Management Information System (MIS)
    D. Both Computer Information System (CIS) and Management Information System (MIS)

True or False

14. All IT careers require the same education level.
    True
    False
15. MIS offers a technical IT degree.
    True
    False
16. Some IT careers are less stressful than other IT careers.
    True
    False
17. Both MIS & CIS offer technical IT degrees.
    True
    False
18. All IT careers are stress free.
    True
    False
19. MIS deals with only technology-related courses.
    True
    False
20. Jobs in a CIS discipline require professionals to have no problem-solving skills.
    True
    False
21. Computer Engineer is a non-technical IT domain.
    True
    False

6

Why Choose a Career in the IT Field?

6.1 Introduction

In the 21st century, technology dictates and governs human beings' lives, including the functioning of organizations. Without technology, organizations cannot carry out their business functions, such as communicating with their suppliers, understanding their customers' needs to develop and sell qualitative products and services, or even operate in the global market. Technological advances have transformed work by decreasing the effect of distance and drastically reducing communication costs. The geographic spread of work is growing as many software companies outsource projects to India or other nations where the salaries are much lower. Organizations can outsource their manufacturing to other geographically distant areas and rely on the Internet to continue business. Employees can now do most of their work from home rather than in an office. With so many advancements and benefits in day-to-day life, it becomes evident that an IT career is in great demand.

Building a career in IT has its perks. Let's consider some of these in the next sections.

6.2 Ever-Changing Industry

In recent years, a considerable number of changes have transpired in the technology industry, leading to a greater demand for well-equipped and skilled workers. With the advent of new technologies such as the Internet, the IT industry will forever grow and generate more jobs and new careers for interested individuals looking to be employed in the field. The field is characterized by change, as any one invention results in yet more advancements. The IT industry is particularly in continuous change, paving the way for numerous possibilities

DOI: 10.1201/9781003204114-6

without bounds. New opportunities continue to appear while existing ones evolve based on the current trends.

The impact of IT advancements on other industries is vast and is moving quickly in the modern era as many solutions are moving into the digital arena. For example, organizations are increasingly opting to move from physical to online environments. This has given rise to online commerce, cloud computing technology, digital libraries, and online learning. Many organizations perceive IT as a convenient method of fostering their activities and operations. The digital transformation, which has sped up due to the rapid changes in innovative technologies, drives the IT industry and fosters the need and demand for new job types. Technological advances have increased people's needs, creating many opportunities to choose from to improve their career and growth. IT growth is felt across different industries and applied in almost every aspect of a business. Thus, by taking up a career in the information technology field, one is assured of growth and development in their skills, knowledge, and expertise.

6.3 High Income

Information technology professionals are paid well compared to other professionals due to the high-level skills required in the field. IT professionals encompass a unique set of skills and knowledge, making them a vital asset of any organization. Because of their worth and value to a business enterprise, they are paid a higher salary for their services. Even though many IT personnel do not earn as much at the beginning of their career, they tend to move up the salary ladder as they advance their careers. This can be further accelerated by acquiring new skills, gaining work experience, or attaining an advanced degree. Compared to other jobs in different industries, IT professionals draw a reasonably large paycheck even for an organization's starting position. For example, the U.S. Bureau of Labor Statistics figures for 2016 indicate that computer programmers earned an average of $79,000. The bottom 10% of programmers earned less than $45,000 and the top 10% earned at least $130,000.

The IT industry jobs do not only offer a secure career with good pay. Individuals who are embarking in the field with little experience and knowledge can find employment. Individuals looking to become employed in the IT industry will not see themselves out of work any time soon. The skills required in these jobs are highly valued and needed within organizations and companies' day-to-day operations. Therefore, by advancing one's skills, knowledge, and expertise in these fields, one is assured of a better income than other professions.

6.4 Low-Cost Education

One of the benefits of pursuing a career in the IT field is that it costs less to earn the requisite education and degrees than other career options. People interested in IT can quickly enroll in courses in a certified IT area and do not necessarily have to spend four years at a college to gain IT experience and knowledge. In contrast to some other high-paying careers, a university degree might not be required to become an IT professional. Graduating from a technical college, obtaining experience through summer internships, and completing certifications in professional courses are reliable alternatives afforded to professionals trying to launch their IT career.

Some people undergo quick training to earn certifications in specific fields of IT to gain technical knowledge. Such certificates let students save significantly on costs they would have otherwise incurred to pay for college tuitions. Earning a certificate in a particular area in IT opens many opportunities. It can land an individual in a higher-paying role, allowing them to fulfill their dreams and realize their full potential in the field. Similarly, it enables students who depend on government loans to manage their loans more efficiently while also removing barriers to middle-class families in providing education for their children.

One can develop a successful professional career in the IT field without needing the time and money to invest in higher-level education like master's or PhD degrees. There are even jobs in the IT field for individuals without a college or university degree. Take the case of web developers, who are required to manage the visual settings and technical content of websites. Even though some will have earned a college degree before landing their job as a web developer, some organizations require prospective employees to have the needed experience but not necessarily a college degree. In other words, without a college degree, an individual can earn a good sum of money per year working as a web developer. Individuals can become a professional IT employee at an organization and enhance their career without spending a large amount of money to earn a master's degree. The low cost of education makes careers in this field attractive and encourages more students to enroll for the courses in the field.

A career in the IT field will depend on the number of certifications individuals obtain and their technical knowledge. If individuals want to advance in their careers, they can earn technical certifications for less. Moreover, with the advent of technology, individuals do not have to attend a physical school to earn an IT education. Many universities and technical institutions offer online options for those who want to study remotely.

Learning any new technology or new programming language is incredibly easy and cheap. For instance, many learning platforms like Udemy, Khan Academy, Eudonix, and so on provide numerous courses taught by highly educated and experienced professors at a low cost. Some courses are even free. Similarly, a video-sharing platform like YouTube has learning videos uploaded by experts and professionals completely free of charge. As IT is a field with continuous growth, more and more knowledge-sharing platforms are helping newcomers learn technical skills from experienced professionals at no cost.

6.5 Job Security

The IT industry is one of the leading industries today since every aspect of human life involves technology use. Consider the example of Amazon online shopping. People want to buy groceries in the market for daily needs like vegetables or fruits. To get these products into the grocery store, we need real-time labor to carry these things to the stores. Now customers want to buy these products either by ordering them online or through reaching out to the store. In the scenario where a customer orders an item online, he may be expecting the item to arrive in a few days. To select items and add them to his virtual cart, the customer either needs a web application or mobile application. Hence, the IT industry will come into the picture. The developer needs to build the code, and the development team needs to identify the path forward to make such transactions possible.

Many teams are involved in building the application, including the management team, development team, and network security team. And this sort of application will have long-term use because its users will continuously buy these products from grocery stores or online applications. This illustrates how the IT industry provides job security to every person who participates in the development of such an application. The selected persons for the development and management process are highly qualified. There will be job security for any individual who has good knowledge about the application and development.

6.6 Learning New Skills

Another reason to choose IT careers is that they provide the opportunity to learn new skills every day. Those who love continuous learning will enjoy the way that IT allows you to start with one tech job and jump to another IT job in the same company if interested. For example, you may take a web development job and want to learn something new and exciting like game design. In that case, you can jump from developing an application to developing games by improving your knowledge set. The acquisition of this diverse knowledge further helps in career growth and keeps you up to date with the changing technology. In addition to technical expertise, other skills acquired through IT careers include strategic thinking, time management, leadership, customer service, industry knowledge, and professionalism.

These skills benefit mental well-being as well as boost your confidence and self-esteem. Thus, it increases future employment opportunities, career growth, satisfaction, and optimism. Skills like coding, networking, time management, and communication skills are essential skills required by all organizations and companies. IT careers can improve all these skills.

For example, a security administrator responsible for IT systems' security can improve knowledge by going through all the latest security news in his aim to better understand current security threats and other security-related information. This not only helps him gain knowledge but also helps in strengthening security. Since most IT jobs provide access to different content types, it will be easy to learn these skills. Furthermore, one can learn at their own pace by enrolling in online tutorials for improving their technical skills. Finally, it is cost-effective to learn these skills as most IT companies either provide free content for their employees to learn or sponsor the IT employees to attend interesting and informative conferences.

6.7 Always in Demand

Information technology provides companies with great flexibility by improving and facilitating access to new products and services. It also allows them to build new products and services themselves. IT enables companies to respond to product and industry trends by utilizing the latest technology and the best available expertise, leading to rapid innovation and paradigm shifts. IT helps companies respond quickly to the ever-changing demands of customers.

Individuals seeking careers in IT have great flexibility in finding employment. They are not bound to specific IT organizations or departments but can work as part of an entire team or as employees in various departments. Their job may extend across many areas of a given company or organization. Most people in IT need to work with multiple applications and projects simultaneously, making IT an ideal career for those who work with various technologies but often do not need to work with all of them.

IT offers a wide range of practical and theoretical research. Furthermore, it provides opportunities to apply knowledge in a wide range of domains, from finance and strategy to security and information technology. Meanwhile, organizations are faced with the increasing need to offer the right product for the right price. Today, it is more important to have what people want and need than ever before, especially given the way that demand has been altered by the Internet. The fast-paced IT industry is highly competitive, and it is critical that the industry excels in innovation, creativity, and cost savings. The need to focus on innovation has caused business managers to create several new leadership training initiatives.

6.8 Job Diversity

Careers in IT provide more job opportunities because the IT industry itself makes advances on such a regular basis. It provides the chance to work in companies and organizations building tools and infrastructure to operate and grow competitively. For example, all businesses and organizations need their software developers and designers to authorize the hardware, software, and applications needed to monitor and benefit their workflow and create innovation. The organization needs individuals who can manage and support the functions and working of the inner IT system. They also require the external support staff to prioritize other IT staff. Similarly, individuals work as a routine staff to support an organization's staff and work, and they work as network staff to reduce the staff's work downtime and provide a more stable working environment. IT offers job opportunities as an external IT staff to collaborate with internal staff to combine their knowledge to offer a wide range of technology solutions.

Businesses also need experts to align and implement solutions that directly align their business strategies. Experts advise the best practices to follow and prevent possible mistakes that can occur while implementing new solutions. Expertise is required to reduce implementation time and thereby save the business time and money. Experts ensure that businesses get the best from their IT investment. Onsite IT professionals are compulsory for any organization in order to ensure that qualified individuals handle any emergencies that require immediate action. Notably, managers need IT developers to research existing technology systems and discover new and better tools enabling them to reach their competitive targets, goals, and objectives.

Diversity is needed in the IT industry so that different IT professionals can interact more effectively without any obstacles. The gender gap is a serious obstacle facing the workforce in many countries, but in the United States problems of gender and race inequity at work show signs of improvement. Gender inequity in the IT industry in particular is less of a problem, and the IT industry doesn't show any inequity across pay value or the structuring in pay scales. As diversity also involves the hiring of the most qualified persons regardless of race or gender, it is also one of the best things the IT industry has when compared to other sectors.

6.9 Chapter Summary

The information technology field is associated with several benefits to individuals, societies, nations, and the world. It has contributed to international trade growth, enhanced communication, and increased employment opportunities as well as enabled its professionals to earn a good income and benefits. However, to succeed in the field, IT professionals need to sharpen their skills, knowledge, and expertise. Many individuals opt for a career in the IT field due to the various advantages compared with other industries.

Chapter Review Questions

1. In one paragraph, explain why IT field continues to grow? Why is it necessary?
2. Why IT career is in great demand? Provide three reasons.

7
Forming an IT Career Plan

7.1 Introduction

Businesses worldwide are now using the latest technologies to stay ahead of their competitors. Consequently, the need for skilled, educated, and capable IT professionals is growing drastically.

The process of carrier planning is time consuming but plays a crucial role in reaching one's target goals within a required timeframe. One may suffer long-term consequences if one does not plan properly. What individuals want to achieve in their life's work is fundamental to who they are. Every individual creates his/her own unique experience that forms their perspective on the world. One's job preferences will be guided in part by his/her previous experiences as well as influenced by his/her environment, mindset, and the resources available to them. An individual's impressions about his/her culture, personality, and resources may affect his/her career choices. One should develop informed and realistic career aspirations to get the most out of his/her studies and reach his/her initial career goals. Career planning in IT is essential as it will help an individual assess and select the right options from among the many sectors in the field, such as software, hardware, networking, and much more.

7.2 Getting Started in Information Technology

Many of those who pursue IT careers are also drawn to the values of teamwork, helping people, overcoming challenges, and positively changing the world. If you are looking for a position that will regularly test you, pay well, and offer opportunities for advancement, a career in information technology is a great place to start. Since IT career options are diverse, the first step to consider is to focus on what

DOI: 10.1201/9781003204114-7

you enjoy or hate about what you are doing *now* and what you want to do *next*. Think about whether you wish to continue in your current direction or take a different one.

When you have settled on a plan of action, write down the steps you need to take along the way. Do your homework and consult with experts in the field to get their guidance. Reflect upon and take note of any shortcomings you will need to address so as not to hinder you from completing your next moves. Identify deficiencies that could make you less marketable as an applicant and seek to strengthen those by networking or obtaining a credential.

7.3 Identify Your Passions

If you are looking for a role that makes you happy, the IT field has specialties from which to select. Research what you feel would be the perfect match for you, determine your own personal interests first, and then seek to satisfy them in the professional sphere. Consider the following questions for yourself:

- What level of interest do I have in IT?
- Why do I think I should try an IT career?
- What do I do on the computer when I am not working?
- Does my browsing background have anything to do with resolving a technological issue?
- Do I like troubleshooting technological problems?
- Do I like learning new things?

Whether it is about ourselves or other people, passion can be difficult to describe and articulate; however, we all acknowledge it when we notice it. Passion is what drives you to conquer challenges and reach your goals.

Today, everything is impacted by technology; hence, many factors go into people's passions when it comes to IT. If you keep up with technology and the pace at which it advances, you may crave to transform this hobby into a profession. As an IT professional, you will help your customers and enable your organization to reach its goals. Businesses depend on IT to help them meet their challenges, making IT professionals indispensable.

7.4 Shorten Your Interest List

Successful self-evaluation helps narrow down your interest list and provides a checklist of your career ambitions. We are all passionate about doing something, but we might have too many passions. Sometimes, our passions may not sustain us, or the passion we have may not suit our professional life. It is quite common for people to possess too many interests and not decide how to focus on just one. With limited time it is impossible to focus on all, so we must narrow them down to spend more time developing expertise in the one or a few that are most important to us.

After you have explored your career interest, you should next research the career itself. The process can be time consuming depending on the field or the current job market. You may want to talk to people who are already in the career, or find volunteer work, internships, or part-time work to gather more information. Your activities in these areas will help you narrow down your interests and determine what you truly care about.

Aligning your passions with your professional life gives you comfort and helps you live a fulfilling and sustainable life. Many people have multiple interests and talents, but emphasizing one or a few is a better use of one's time. Being resilient and persistent in a particular interest can lead to success. Developing a personal philosophy will guide you toward your goal and keep you on track. Engaging in multiple activities such as internships, volunteer work, and freelancing might help you focus on one thing.

7.5 Network

We live in a social world where our lives require interacting with other people. Building relationships in IT is vital to succeeding in your career. Networking is the most powerful way to further your progress in your career. In the sense of career growth, networking helps you form relationships to assist you in achieving your career goals. Via networking, people share advice and knowledge relevant to resumes, cover letters, job search strategies, and events or seminars.

Networking can happen in physical or virtual spaces and can happen anytime. Remember that each new partnership you form extends your network, and this in turn gets you closer to success. There are a number of networking techniques to use that can be highly effective. Let's consider some of these in the next section.

7.6 Networking Techniques

Professional organizations. Professional organizations host meetings, conferences, and activities that will be attended by important people in the field. For example, you can find out more about companies such as the Association for Computing Machinery (ACM), the world's largest academic and informational computing society. If you become a member, you can gain access to professionals with whom to connect and build your professional network.

Volunteering. Even if you volunteer outside of your profession, volunteering can lead to meeting new people who can help you advance in your career. Interacting with others and pursuing shared interests allow you to keep contacts that can benefit you in the future. Several companies offer students paid and unpaid internships to help them develop essential skills for their profession as well as the opportunity to meet new people.

Expert experience. You can reach out to people in your chosen field and seek their expertise and experience. Experienced professionals can help you in your own progress by sharing how they chose their field and what makes them successful.

Part-time employment. While full-time employment is your main goal, filling in some gaps with a part-time job could help you find associates and contacts who can assist your professional network. It also enables you to gain valuable knowledge along the way, which can be used on your curriculum vitae.

7.7 Build a Robust Curriculum Vitae

Your curriculum vitae (CV) demonstrates to employers that you have the required expertise to do the job. To prepare for an IT career, you will need a solid CV that accurately reflects your skills. Detail all acquired education, experiences, internships, achievements, and anything relevant to your role.

Building a good CV requires examining the job requirements and learning about the organization. This will give you the knowledge to add information that is essential to the work since recruiters often have little time to review a CV. During your interview, you will be given a chance to expand on any skills that were not included in your CV.

7.8 Go on the Job Hunt

Job hunting is a vital aspect of a reliable career plan in IT. There are different types of jobs that are categorized under IT, so understanding the different types is crucial. Payment scale and the overall objectivity of a given job are key factors to observe while conducting a job hunt in IT. Before applying for a job, it is essential to understand the job type as well as its required skills, functions, and duties.

A professional IT expert can help you to find the right direction in job searching. They can provide sound knowledge about expanding your knowledge and how it can apply to your profession. It is essential to know what kind of questions might be asked in an interview. A person might need to practice discussing information security, for instance, to help him or her to do well in an interview. Before you apply for a job, it is always essential to determine which job characteristics relate to your passion. If your interests are not related to your job, it will just be a waste of your time and it will not give you the satisfaction you want to achieve through your professional work.

Social media platforms such as Facebook, Instagram, and WhatsApp can be good sources of job listings. LinkedIn is the biggest platform for job advertisements. Here you can find only work-related posts to help build your profession. Based on an individual's qualifications, it remains highly essential to cross-check all IT jobs at your disposal and make the right decisions about the most promising ones. This eventually translates into job satisfaction and general career growth.

7.9 Chapter Summary

As technology continues to advance there will be an increased demand for IT-skilled professionals who can help take business and organizations to the next level. If an individual plans to embark on an IT career, he/she must choose a career plan that entails organizing a training path and setting goals. Many organizations provide training on various IT skills via online videos. Individuals can utilize such services to acquire the required knowledge to execute their job duties and plan for certifications as part of developing their CV.

Information technology is the best career option for reasons such as good pay, career stability, and positive work and life balance. The wide range of jobs in the IT field allows people to choose any type of job they are interested in. Producing a good career plan, committing oneself to learning, and adapting to technological changes can help you achieve career goals. By choosing an IT career, you also help society as everything in today's world runs on technology. A career in IT will offer growth potential and an excellent opportunity to turn your talents and passions into a career.

Chapter Review Questions

1. Why is career planning in IT essential and crucial?
2. Name two considerations when forming an IT Career Plan.
3. A career in IT will offer growth potential and an excellent opportunity to turn your talent into a career. Do you agree or disagree with this statement? Why and why not?

8

Information Technology and Society

8.1 Introduction

Advances in technology have changed the ways we learn and conduct our daily lives. IT now touches every sector of society and is integrated in such a way that we can enjoy it in all places and contexts. Think about cars with built-in satellite navigation, for instance, and about the digital displays within them. IT has also enabled us to see and visit other places without having to be physically present. For example, people in Africa can watch in real time a soccer event in Europe without having to be physically present at that event. Mobile devices have changed the way people communicate and enabled them to perform tasks more quickly and more flexibly than ever before. More and more companies seek to expand and enhance their use of IT to gain the edge needed to outsmart, outpace, and out-deliver their competitors. In healthcare, education, security, and other sectors of society, productivity and outcomes cannot be optimized without using information technology.

8.2 Business

No matter the size of a business organization, technology has substantial effects on business operations. The fundamental idea of business is to generate profits by selling products or services. In business, information technology allows people to do more work in a shorter amount of time. Faster communication, electronic storage, and records protection are some of the advantages afforded by information technology to business.

For example, a business like Amazon simplifies how customers do their grocery shopping using information technology. Just a few clicks

DOI: 10.1201/9781003204114-8

on a website allow customers to submit an order while IT sends that order to the company. By deploying IT, a business can optimize operations and resource utilization, thereby creating more business profits. IT can be used to automate routine tasks that help a business to operate efficiently. By leveraging various tools, IT helps to understand market demands, provides new business opportunities, and helps in business expansion.

IT's role in business is seen in how it can help an organization increase performance, improve customer experience, save money, streamline communications, and enhance manager decision-making. For instance, online meetings and video conferencing platforms, such as Zoom, Skype, and GoToMeeting, enable business organizations to collaborate virtually in real time. This, in turn, reduces costs associated with bringing participants onsite. IT allows a business to virtually travel into new markets without the cost and risks of creating a physical trip or factory at another location. The goal of adapting IT in a business is to increase business profits, make business management more manageable, and protect the business from various threats.

8.3 Education

Information technology has fostered new avenues for learning. For example, using the Internet, people can access educational materials from the comfort of their own chosen locations. We can get any information from our homes whenever we need it. Books, journals, articles, newspapers, and more are available and easily accessible via the Internet, thereby enabling us to have ample access to resources when we need them regardless of our locations.

8.3.1 E-Learning

In recent decades, e-learning has evolved as an area of particular interest. E-learning is a form of learning which takes place online via the Internet. Such an interactive process enables teachers to teach while students learn from the comfort of their respective locations. Today, you can have a student residing in Liberia while attending a university in California. All that the students will need to complete their program will be the necessary hardware and software (i.e., a computer, internet connection, and access to a digital library). Whatever the process, there is always a teacher interacting and grading students' participation, quizzes, tests, assignments, and discussion forums, making e-learning a convenient way to learn.

8.3.2 Digital Library

Information technology makes digital libraries (DL) possible. DL is indispensable for education as it offers a wide range of sources and up-to-date materials with immediate online access. In a digital library, learning can be an independent process as it provides a wide range of readily available online educational resources, making learning possible. The effective integration of IT in education helps make teaching and learning more meaningful and fun. You can have teacher-to-students and student-to-student collaboration through technological applications.

8.4 Communication

Information technology has increased globalization. There is a growing interdependence of the world economies and cultures, making it possible for information to be shared quickly and easily from all over the globe without the barriers of language and geography. Today's business environment makes it a must for businesses to interact with customers quickly and clearly. IT plays a major role in how businesses interact with customers. For example, websites allow customers to find answers to their questions twenty-four seven and quickly. This gives confidence to the customers and creates a more positive public image for the business.

Let's look more closely at the example of communication as it has changed our daily lives. Unlike in the past, where we communicated via post-marked writing, we now communicate using information networks like mobile phones, social media, the Internet, and so on. It is cheaper to make a phone call to another person in Europe than to send a letter. The emergence of the social media age has made it possible for people from different parts of the world to share a platform to exchange messages, images, and videos in real time. Social media means that no part of the world is isolated from another as people are continually being updated on what is happening in different parts of the world.

8.5 Healthcare

The most notable use of IT in healthcare involves inpatient records and data management. In the past, healthcare professionals used clunky paper charts that could be easily lost, damaged, or misinterpreted. Now, providers can track patient records securely and efficiently, append pharmacy records, test results, perform X-rays, and even record vital signs to a virtual chart that is easier to read and share and can also be checked against other databases.

Moreover, nursing informatics has sprung up at the intersection of clinical care and information technology. This interdisciplinary study links together nursing practice with the management of IT. The field is growing ever more popular with increased demand in technology and a workforce that wants to combine their passions for science and data in service to medical patients and improved healthcare for all. As people are always seeking quality care, the demand for IT that can accurately track patients and improve healthcare is expected to grow.

Expect more IT professional jobs in hospital settings as the field expands. Healthcare IT roles are growing every year, from record technicians to medical coding specialists, transcriptionists, healthcare information engineers, and clinical IT consultants. IT will stay relevant for hospital administrators looking to increase the volume, speed, and quality of service in their care centers.

8.6 Banking and Finance

Information technology has changed the banking sector and the ways we bank. Online banking is perhaps one of the most significant changes that have ever happened in the banking sector. For example, customers can quickly move money by just keying in their account details online to access their bank account. This allows for the easy, quick transfer and management of their finances virtually and from anywhere.

Information technology has changed the way we buy things. Unlike before, where cash was the primary way of making purchases, today, we can purchase using a debit or credit card with chip and PIN. It has made our lives so much easier. ATM machines allow us to dispense money on the spot whenever we need it. Another significant change that has been brought about by IT is the globalization of the banking sector. Today, a customer in New York with "Bank A" can carry on a financial transaction with "Bank B" in Liberia. Banks throughout the world now enjoy a global presence and can transact from anywhere at any time. They can operate across the globe, making it possible for them to share data quickly and conveniently. Even with these advances, the most significant revolution could still be yet to come.

8.7 Security

With so many transactions done online and so much information available online, it is crucial to keep all that safe. Businesses are subject to various security threats, including cybercrimes, vandalism, and others. The use of IT can help protect financial data, confidential executive decisions, and other proprietary information that is vital to competition. With information technology hardware, along with the necessary software, online business data can stay secure until accessed by authorized personnel. Businesses can ensure that the competitors will steal none of their past or future project ideas.

Law enforcement uses IT to make their jobs safer and more effective. For example, law enforcement uses the Internet to identify, find, and follow criminals. The Internet is also being used to obtain evidence to bring charges against and help to prosecute criminals.

Similarly, law enforcement uses IT to make possible predictive policing. Predictive policing involves the use of computer systems to develop policing strategies based on geospatial statistics and fact-based intervention models to reduce crime and improve public safety. This practice can focus on factors that affect crime rates in particular locations. Hence, predictive policing practices also invite criticism insofar as it can reinforce existing biases against minorities. So, law enforcement personnel using such a technology should be made aware of how to detect and avoid such biases. These actions are making police work safer for both themselves and the people they protect.

8.8 Research

The work of research involves writing proposals, designing experiments, collecting data, analyzing data, and communicating findings to the public. Information technology has significant effects on all these activities. For example, researchers can use Facebook, LinkedIn, or Qualtrics to collect data and utilize google documents to share the information. A business with the technological capacity to research new opportunities will have a competitive advantage as acquiring new opportunities allows a business to grow and survive.

8.9 How IT Professionals Fit into Society

Though information technology plays a significant role in our daily lives, advances in the field will not happen without IT professionals to set them in place. That is why studying IT is very rewarding. Remember, as discussed in Chapter 3, IT professionals are equipped with IT knowledge, skills, and techniques.

As an IT professional, you will be responsible for performing various tasks like building, testing, repairing, and maintaining different hardware and software products that form a complex network of computer systems. As an IT professional, your main aim is to live up to the industry's expectations, the clients, and the general public. It is good to keep in mind that as the IT industry grows, more complex technological systems will evolve. The IT professional's role is vital, so the demand for well-qualified IT professionals is always on the rise.

8.10 Chapter Summary

This chapter introduced students to the important role that information technology plays in our society. IT is important in every aspect of our lives. Whether in our way of communicating, banking, conducting research, or learning, we need IT to make our jobs easier and more efficient. For advances in IT to continue, we need people to continue entering and studying the field.

Chapter Review Questions

1. What are some of the importance of IT in your community?
2. What are some of the impacts of Information Technology on education?
3. What are some of the impacts of Information Technology on healthcare?
4. How does IT help us in our communication processes?
5. Name four ways IT can help create jobs?
6. Name and explain two ways IT helps the healthcare industry.
7. Explain how IT has changed education.

True or False

8. IT has no impact on people's lives.
   True
   False

Fill in the Blanks

9. ________is accessing learning electronically.

9
Future Trends in IT

9.1 Introduction

With technology becoming more advanced and requiring faster speeds, IT will need to make sure we can navigate these different technologies without slowing down. Future trends in IT demonstrate why people must equip themselves with basic information technology knowledge. The coming decades are likely to produce exciting technological advances that will further transform the world and how people live and interact. Some important future trends in IT include artificial intelligence, the Internet of Things (IoT), and others.

9.2 Future Trends in IT

The pace at which rapidly evolving technology enables change and progress will become exponential. More recently, the Coronavirus (COVID-19) pandemic has made it much clearer that how the role of IT professionals will not stay the same in a continuously evolving and contactless world. Since COVID-19, many of us have been forced to work or do our schoolwork from home. This means that we must have a good internet signal and a good working computer to keep the same efficiency level as we would in a traditional work or school setting. IT helps us accomplish this goal. It is essential for staying current with new technology trends and focusing on the future to know which skills to acquire to secure a safe job. The next sections discuss in more detail a few of the top technology trends to watch for.

9.2.1 Artificial Intelligence

Artificial Intelligence (AI) is among the most critical future IT trends. AI is a part of computer science that concentrates on automated machines that think, work, and respond like humans. Rather than

DOI: 10.1201/9781003204114-9

serving as a replacement for human intelligence and ingenuity, AI serves as a supporting tool. For example, businesses use AI-powered chatbots to provide twenty-four seven customer care services, automatically resolve questions without any human intervention, and provide support to multiple customers at once. Chatbots, unlike humans, do not need sleep. If your team is unavailable, a chatbot can step in to answer questions and provide links to resources. But if the bot cannot help, it can still indicate available hours when a human will next be in touch. The increasing ability of machines to learn and act intelligently will transform our world.

9.2.2 5G

The fifth generation of wireless technology (5G) will profoundly impact our lives more than any technology since the Internet because 5G enables us to realize the potential of a fully connected world. For example, data-based voice calls or video calls (like Skype) will not experience any delay time or failure. In terms of mobile connectivity, 5G technology can allow one to stream a movie while traveling by train with the same quality as if watching it at home. In the medical field, 5G networks will make remote surgical procedures or even wireless healthcare a reality. 5G speed significantly outpaces previous networks, allowing the businesses to reach consumers through faster, smarter, and more stable wireless networking. 5G redefines networks and establishes a new global wireless standard for speed, throughput, and bandwidth. A 5G technology builds a bridge to the future.

9.2.3 Driverless Cars

Artificial intelligence is beginning to make possible what was once considered impossible, as in the case of driverless cars. Driverless vehicles can control and guide themselves without human control. In the next couple of years, these vehicles will be commercially available in the market on a large scale. To become fully autonomous, driverless cars will need to communicate with the other cars in traffic to avoid accidents and minimize congestion. Driverless vehicles will need to communicate with driverless cars, traffic lights, embedded sensors, and road signs. These will require instant responses for which the low-latency 5G networks come in. This technology will impact the transportation industry as there will no longer be issues such as driver strikes.

9.2.4 Internet of Things

The Internet of Things (IoT) is another possible information technology trend in the future. It is a concept that has the potential to impact how we live and work. But what is the IoT and its impact on you, if any? Due to the many complexities around the IoT, let's stick to the basics. As broadband Internet becomes widely available, the cost of connecting decreases. The creation of more Wi-Fi-capable devices, a significant reduction in technology costs, and a rise in smartphone penetration create a perfect storm for the IoT.

Simply put, IoT is the concept of connecting any device with an on-and-off switch to the Internet. This includes everything from cell phones, headphones, lamps, and almost anything else you can think of. If it has an on-and-off switch, chances are it can be a part of the IoT.

The new rule for the future would be such that any connectable thing will be connected. For example, suppose you are going to a meeting but you are running late. Your car could already know the fastest route to take. Based on the traffic condition, your car might send a text to the other party notifying them that you will be late.

On a broader scale, the IoT allows for virtually endless opportunities and connections to occur, many of which we cannot even think of or fully understand. It is not hard to see how and why the IoT is such a hot topic today as it certainly opens the door to many opportunities.

9.2.5 Digital Platforms

Social media has and will continue to become an integral part of our lives. Social media started as a communication channel between friends and family but now consists of multi-billion-dollar platforms that greatly influence people's lives. Facebook, for example, is the biggest social network worldwide with over billions of users. Communication methods on Facebook, such as chats, messaging, comments, wall posts, and pokes, are important ways to exchange information. On a cultural level, this kind of popularity represents a capacity to shape language and, in turn, shapes users' communication methods.

Social media is also a channel for businesses to connect with their customers through well-crafted social media strategies. Companies use social media sites as a medium to advertise products. This has become a source for people to learn more about products and services, organizations, and world events. Marketing on social media sites can exhibit a viral effect. Information shared spreads exponentially among the targeted users from the billions of users. As people's addiction to their digital identities and social media usage continues to deepen, so too will these trends in their social lives.

9.2.6 Remote Work

There is an increase in the number of people opting to work from home (i.e., work remotely) instead of following the traditional model of being physically present at a particular location. This has led to more flexibility and productivity in the workplace and helped people sustain more than one job. It has also exposed both workers and consumers to the global marketplace. Businesses can choose to hire top professionals from anywhere globally and are no longer limited to locals. For example, a New York-based company may employ an IT analyst situated in South Africa without requiring the individual to be physically present in New York. In the case of a pandemic, working remotely can help prevent the spread of illness. This saves businesses by avoiding lost productivity and protecting their employees and public health in general. For example, the COVID-19 prompted many companies to embrace all employees' remote work. This helped to limit the spread of the virus.

Communication tools such as Slack, GoToMeeting, Skype, and Zoom enable people to get their work done as if they were in a physical office building. Sometimes, meetups are held a couple of times a year to establish a face-to-face connection and strengthen employees working relationships. Overall, as IT advances, work flexibility will be embraced and will be far more advanced. Artificial intelligence and 5G technology will likely play a significant role in remote work and managing remote staff.

9.3 Chapter Summary

From the analysis, it is evident that information technology has played and will continue to play a critical role in improving our quality of life on this planet. Thanks to information technology, human beings can communicate and move from one place to another more quickly than in the past. The cost of communication and transportation has also been reduced. IT in the realm of communication will advance and gain features that make the user experience easier and more appealing. IoT technology will grow and play improved roles in the life of an average user. Artificial intelligence will become sophisticated enough to predict routines and increase the productivity of users across the world.

Future trends indicate a world that will be dominated by information technology. Therefore, individuals must arm themselves with the necessary IT skills to take advantage of future opportunities. There is no doubt that IT will have to be fully adopted by everyone worldwide. IT will make life easier for people and will allow businesses to grow at a faster pace. Everyone needs to understand information technology and appreciate its impact on their lives.

Glossary

Access Points: act as a terminal to provide (mostly wireless) network access

Application software: is designed to benefit users to perform tasks.

Central Processing Unit (CPU): is the bridge between the hardware and software.

Data: is the raw material like numbers or words

Graphics card: processes images and videos.

Gateway: connects two or more networks that use different protocols

Hardware: is the physical part of a computer.

Hard Disk: stores data.

Hub: Connects multiple computer networking devices

Information: is processed data on which our decisions and actions are based.

Information Technology: is the use of systems (telecommunications and computers) for storing, retrieving, and sending information.

Internet: is what people use to share information and communicate from anywhere with an internet connection.

Keyboard: provides commands to the computer and input text.

LAN: connects a small number of computer systems in a relatively close geographical area.

Modern: responsible for establishing a connection to send and receive data over telephone or cable line.

Monitor: is a computer hardware component used to display the videos and output.

Mouse: is a hand-held pointing device that detects two-dimensional motion relative to the screen.

Networks: are basically connections between multiple hardware devices.

Networking Devices: expand the reach, search, and access of a network.

Network Interface Card (NIC): allows the computer to connect and interact with other Local Area Network devices.

Network Operating System: is used to support network resources and ensure that computers communicate efficiently and effectively.

Network Topology: refers to how the devices in a network are arranged to allow communication between the devices.

Open System Interconnection (OSI): provides a conceptual framework for organizing diverse network resources.

Operating System (OS): controls and manages the hardware and other software on the hardware.

Random-Access Memory (RAM): is used to store and process information.

Router: connectivity device used to connect two LANs.

Software: instructs the hardware what to do, when and how to do it.

Switch: generally involves a more intelligent role than hubs —connects other Ethernet devices.

WAN: connects more than one LAN over a considerable geographic distance.

Answer Key

Chapter 1

8. C
9. B
10. B
11. B
12. D
13. C
14. D
15. False
16. False
17. False
18. True
19. False
20. False
21. True
22. False
23. Information
24. Data
25. Information Technology
26. E-Learning
27. Internet

28. World Wide Web
29. Internet
30. Hardware & Network

Chapter 2

1. D
2. True
3. False
4. False
5. True
6. True
7. Hardware
8. Hardware

Chapter 3

11. D
12. B
13. A, C, D
14. C
15. A
16. A
17. Software
18. Operating system and application software
19. Operating system
20. System Software
21. Application Software
22. Hardware
23. Software
24. Operating systems
25. Software
26. Software

Chapter 4

9. B
10. B
11. C
12. B
13. False
14. False
15. False
16. True
17. True
18. True
19. Networks
20. LAN

Chapter 5

10. D
11. C
12. B
13. B
14. False
15. False
16. True
17. False
18. False
19. False
20. False
21. False

Chapter 8

8. False
9. e-learning

Index

Page numbers in *italics* denote figures; those in **bold** denote tables